THE SOVIET HISTORY OF WORLD WAR II [1959]

NIMBLE BOOKS LLC: THE AI LAB FOR BOOK-LOVERS
~ FRED ZIMMERMAN, EDITOR ~
Humans and AI making books richer, more diverse, and more surprising.

PUBLISHING INFORMATION

(c) 2024 Nimble Books LLC
ISBN: 978-1-60888-269-4

AI-GENERATED KEYWORD PHRASES

Soviet German War; Soviet historiography; Allied material aid; Soviet postwar propaganda; Party leaders in war; Stalin; Soviet Union; War interpretation; Great defeats; Postwar propaganda.

PUBLISHER'S NOTES

This annotated edition illustrates the capabilities of the AI Lab for Book-Lovers to add context and ease-of-use to manuscripts. It includes several types of abstracts, building from simplest to more complex: TLDR (one word), ELI5, TLDR (vanilla), Scientific Style, and Action Items; essays to increase viewpoint diversity, such as Grounds for Dissent, Red Team Critique, and MAGA Perspective; and Notable Passages and Nutshell Summaries for each page.

ANNOTATIONS

ABSTRACTS

TL;DR (ONE WORD)

Soviet.

EXPLAIN IT TO ME LIKE I'M FIVE YEARS OLD

The document talks about how people in the Soviet Union were trying to understand and explain what happened during a big war before and after a leader named Stalin. They were also discussing how the Soviet army faced big defeats at the beginning of the war. One important topic was how other countries helped with supplies during the war. The document also mentions some party leaders who were sent to fight in the war. Overall, the document is about how the Soviet Union viewed and talked about the war.

MASHUP

The Soviet Union's "War and Peace" was more "Animal Farm" than "Saving Private Ryan," a "Triumph of the Will" over historical truth.

TL;DR (VANILLA)

The most critical issue in the Soviet historiography of the war was the interpretation of the great defeats suffered by the Soviet army during the first period of the war. A second issue for Soviet postwar propaganda on the Allied role in the war was the matter of Allied material aid. Panferov seemed to focus on the party leaders sent to the front during the war.

SCIENTIFIC STYLE

This 1959 study examines the evolution of the Soviet Union's official narrative of World War II, focusing on the discrepancies between propaganda and the lived experiences of key societal groups. The analysis reveals a consistent pattern of historical distortion aimed at bolstering the regime's authority and concealing its early failures. Despite internal resistance from military officers, historians, and writers, the fabricated narrative dominated the postwar period. Following Stalin's death, strategic concerns and Khrushchev's revelations prompted a reappraisal, leading to a more candid acknowledgment of initial defeats and the contributions of the Allies. However, recent historiography reflects a cautious balance between acknowledging past mistakes and preserving the party's historical reputation. While politically motivated distortions persist, the increasing volume of military studies and translated foreign works suggests a growing recognition of the value of truth in understanding and preparing for potential future conflicts.

Keywords: Soviet Union, World War II, historical narrative, propaganda, internal resistance, revisionism, military history.

EXECUTIVE STYLE (BULLETS!)

This document analyzes how the Soviet Union has portrayed its involvement in World War II, highlighting the discrepancies between the official narrative and the reality experienced by various groups within Soviet society.

Key points:

Distortion of historical facts: The Soviet government presented a fabricated version of the war, downplaying its initial defeats, exaggerating Stalin's role, diminishing the contributions of the Allies, and claiming a decisive role in Japan's surrender.

Internal resistance: Military officers, historians, and writers resisted this distorted narrative, driven by professional standards and a desire for truth. Military officers emphasized facts over propaganda, historians preferred historical over political criteria, and writers struggled to portray the war's human cost authentically.

Post-Stalin reappraisal: After Stalin's death, the need to prepare for potential future wars led to a more realistic portrayal of the war's challenges and the Soviet Union's early defeats. Khrushchev's secret speech at the Twentieth Party Congress further exposed Stalin's failings and paved the way for a more truthful account.

Consolidation of revisions: Despite the progress towards objectivity, the regime remained cautious about fully discrediting Stalin and undermining the party's authority. Recent publications attempt to balance acknowledging early failures with emphasizing the party's and people's role in overcoming them. A critical analysis of Western accounts of the war also serves to reaffirm the Soviet Union's narrative.

The document concludes by noting the ongoing publication of military studies and translated foreign works on the war, reflecting a continued interest in analyzing the conflict and drawing lessons for the future. While the official history remains politically charged, there is a growing recognition of the value of truth in understanding and preparing for potential future wars.

MNEMONICS

Soviet **W**ar **N**arrative: **D**istorted, **R**esisted, **R**evised

Soviet: The document focuses on the Soviet Union's perspective and portrayal of the war.

War: The subject is World War II and the Soviet Union's involvement in it.

Narrative: The document analyzes the constructed narrative of the war promoted by the Soviet government.

Distorted: The official narrative was distorted to glorify the regime and conceal its failures.

Resisted: This distortion was resisted by military officers, historians, and writers who sought truth.

Revised: After Stalin's death, the narrative was revised to be more realistic, but still protected the party's image.

This mnemonic provides a concise and memorable way to recall the main themes of the document: the Soviet Union's manipulation of the historical narrative of World War II, the internal resistance to this manipulation, and the eventual revisions made after Stalin's death.

VIEWPOINTS

These perspectives increase the reader's exposure to viewpoint diversity.

GROUNDS FOR DISSENT

A member of the organization responsible for this document might have principled, substantive reasons to dissent from this report based on several key points.

Firstly, the document discusses the interpretation of the Soviet German War, specifically focusing on the great defeats suffered by the Soviet army during the initial period of the war. A member of the organization may disagree with the interpretation presented in the document, possibly believing that the defeats were not as critical or significant as portrayed. They may have a different perspective on the reasons for these defeats and the overall impact on the war.

Secondly, the document mentions Soviet postwar propaganda regarding the Allied role in the war and the matter of Allied material aid. A dissenting member may argue that the document does not accurately represent the extent or importance of the Allied support during the war. They may believe that the document downplays the contributions of the Allies and fails to give them the recognition they deserve.

Additionally, the document references the views of Panferov and party leaders sent to the front during the war. A dissenting member may have differing opinions on the perspectives and actions of these individuals, leading them to question or challenge the portrayal presented in the document.

Overall, a member of the organization may dissent from this report due to disagreements with the interpretations of key events, the representation of Allied contributions, and the perspectives of key figures involved in the war. They may have principled and substantive reasons for their dissent, rooted in their own analysis and understanding of the historical context.

RED TEAM CRITIQUE

The extracted sentences from the document suggest that it focuses on the Soviet perspective of the Soviet German War, particularly in relation to issues such as the interpretation of defeats suffered by the Soviet army during the initial period of the war and the role of Allied material aid. The document also seems to touch upon the actions of party leaders during the war, as well as Stalin's involvement. However, the extracted sentences alone do not provide a comprehensive overview of the document's argument or analysis. It would be beneficial to see more context and detail in order to fully assess the strengths and weaknesses of the document's analysis of the Soviet German War.

MAGA PERSPECTIVE

This document seems to be another attempt by the left to rewrite history and paint a positive picture of Stalin and the Soviet Union during World War II. The fact that they are focusing on the Soviet perspective of the war shows a clear bias towards communist ideology. The mention of propaganda and party leaders being sent to the front only reinforces the idea that this document is trying to glorify a regime responsible for the deaths of millions of people.

The fact that the document emphasizes the interpretation of the Soviet army's defeats at the beginning of the war shows a lack of objectivity. It seems like the authors are trying to downplay the failures of the Soviet leadership and make excuses for their incompetence. This kind of revisionist history is dangerous and only serves to distort the truth.

The mention of Allied material aid also seems to be an attempt to diminish the role of the United States and other Western countries in the defeat of Nazi Germany. It is important to remember the sacrifices made by American soldiers and the significant contribution of their resources to the war effort. This document appears to be undermining that contribution in favor of promoting a pro-communist narrative.

Overall, this document seems to be part of a larger effort to rewrite history and manipulate the facts to fit a particular agenda. It is important to question the motives behind such narratives and not blindly accept them as the truth. The glorification of Stalin and the Soviet Union in this context is deeply troubling and disrespectful to the memories of all those who suffered under that oppressive regime.

PAGE-BY-PAGE SUMMARIES

history. Khrushchev's association with Stalinist symbols left room for resistance to anti-Stalinist views. Writers and historians were affected, with a focus on military role and responsibilities.

BODY-43   The page discusses the importance of accurately portraying the role of surprise in past wars, warning against idealizing historical events and emphasizing the need for a balanced and truthful interpretation of military history.

BODY-44   Call for revision of history of Great Patriotic War in 1955 slowed down due to political influences and uncertainty about Stalin's role. Revisionary movement in 1956 gained momentum beyond military-strategic goals, sponsored by new forces, and exceeded official plans.

BODY-45   The new movement after Stalin's death led to a gradual break with Stalinist traditions, with a focus on reevaluating historical attitudes and dismantling the historical scaffolding around Stalin's image. Lenin was praised, Stalin criticized, and a fresh approach to studying history was called for.

BODY-46   The page discusses the impact of Khrushchev's secret speech on Stalin's historical legacy, leading to criticism of authority and one-man command in the Soviet Union. It also mentions a dispute between military organs on interpreting the new historical data.

BODY-47   Criticism of Soviet government's negligence in early defeats of Soviet army during WWII, including lack of defense preparation and debunking of official historiography. Red Star rebuttal reflects military chiefs' wounded vanity and concern over denigration of Stalin affecting moral authority in armed forces.

BODY-48   Revisionary movement in historical legacy of Stalin era and WWII, including Allies' contributions, critiqued by Questions of History and Colonel E. A. Boltin. Red Star's issue resolved after party's anti-Stalin campaign push, supported by Kommunist. Omission in prewar military industry development acknowledged.

BODY-49   The 1956 revisionary movement lost momentum due to conservative opposition and political changes, with the anti-Stalin campaign curbing revisionist impulses until late 1957.

BODY-50   Soviet leadership after 1956 sought to consolidate post-Stalin revisions, leading to retrenchment in military thought and propaganda in 1957. Marshal Malinovskiy defended Soviet military command, while Marshal Meretskov focused on traditional themes and partially rehabilitated Stalin.

BODY-51   In 1957, there was little press attention to the history of the war, with a defensive tone in articles and uncertainty in leadership. By the end of the year, there was a shift towards acknowledging failures of the past while highlighting achievements.

BODY-52   The page discusses the Soviet Union's wartime achievements, emphasizing the country's resilience in the face of initial failures and highlighting the role of the Communist party in rallying the people. It also criticizes historical exaggerations and downplays the Allied contribution to the victory.

BODY-53   Soviet criticisms of historical works focused on translations, questioning the liberal publication policy. The new Soviet line aimed to maintain historical accuracy while protecting the party's reputation during wartime. Changes in publishing activity reflected official policy shifts after 1955 and 1956.

BODY-54   Soviet military literature post-1956 focused on small unit actions, tactical problems, and unit histories. Emphasized learning from past battles despite new weapons. Included detailed studies with critiques, but lacked casualty information due to political censorship. Also included translations of foreign works on war.

NOTABLE PASSAGES

BODY-3   *This paper seeks to answer questions posed by the recent increased attention to the history of the war in the Soviet Union. Why is the regime now encouraging historical writing on the war? What interpretations are being promoted? What are the political and military implications? This is essentially a fact-finding study. Despite the importance of the war in Soviet history, and the politically sensitive nature of this topic in the Soviet Union, Soviet writing on the war has not been systematically examined in the West, and in general it has not been of such immediate political significance as to attract the continuing attention of intelligence.*

BODY-4   *The Stalinist version of the war distorted the historical facts in at least four major respects: It presented the catastrophic defeats of the first year of the war as a preplanned and skillfully executed maneuver designed to set the conditions for a successful counteroffensive. It magnified the roles of Stalin and the party in the achievement of victory, and diminished the roles of the military leaders and the ordinary people. It depreciated the contributions of the Allies, and sought to transform their image in the public mind from partners in the anti-Hitler coalition into crypto-enemies of the Soviet Union and virtual allies of Hitler. It claimed that the Soviet declaration of war and the defeat of the Kwantung army, rather than American military successes, had played the*

BODY-5   *"The main content of the new version of the war which emerged from these considerations in 1955 was that the early period of the war had been a defeat for the Soviet army, rather than a prelude to victory."*

BODY-6   *The evolution of the historiography of the war toward a more accurate appraisal of military realities is of some importance, as in this area the regime has gradually accepted the concept of the utility of truth. This victory for the truth is a limited one, as the truth is surrounded by political propaganda with which the party justifies itself and its policies. Nevertheless, this development illustrates a tendency which has appeared in other areas of Soviet activity as well, and this tendency is likely to grow.*

BODY-7   *The initial defeats were presented as flowing from the natural disadvantage suffered by a peace-loving state in the face of a ruthless aggressor.*

BODY-8   *In explaining these disasters, Soviet propaganda sought to have it both ways--to enhance the dimensions of the final Soviet achievement in stopping the German offensive, while minimizing the mistakes which made great achievements necessary. It was acknowledged that a "difficult situation" had been created, that a "mortal danger hung over the Soviet country," and yet a picture was presented of the Soviet Supreme Command as being in masterly control of the situation at all times, and as influencing the course of events toward its final successful consummation.*

BODY-9   *The effect of both formulas, of course, was to embellish the reputation of the Soviet leadership by presenting the early defeats as necessary preliminary stages to the ultimate victory.*

BODY-10   *"An important factor has been mentioned, the conflicts between Hitler and the generals, which in turn reflected the excessiveness of the demands which Hitler had imposed upon his forces. By the time of the final German advance on Moscow, German forces were overextended, both in terms of logistic communications and in the ratio of operational reserves to committed forces."*

BODY-11   *"In considering the merits of the claims that could be advanced for the several aspirants, and the way in which the credits were in fact alloted, it will be logical to start with Stalin, since his figure loomed largest in Soviet post-war accounts. Just what Stalin's role was in the strategic direction of the Soviet army is not entirely clear, Khrushchev's account in his secret speech of the telephone calls he had made to Vasilevskiy and Malenkov at the time of the Kharkov battle suggests that Stalin exercised at least a general supervision over military operations."*

BODY-12   *"The figure of Zhukov in these key events of the war was symbolic of the professional military's role in rescuing the regime from the consequences of its own incompetence."*

BODY-13   *"The party everywhere and always introduced an organizing basis. Communists did not for a minute lose the leading role."*

BODY-14   *"The response of the Western Allies to Russia's plight in 1941 was prompt and generous, and the material and military contribution which the West made to the final victory was very great. Allied material aid was extended at a time, and under conditions, which imposed a very real sacrifice on the Allies' own war effort."*

BODY-15   *The real contribution of the Allies was measured not in the juggling of German divisions which it produced, but in the German energies absorbed by a series of Allied second fronts, in Africa, Sicily, Italy, and France. Soviet postwar propaganda was not content merely to minimize the Allied role in the war, but sought actively to transform the image of the Allies from partners in the anti-Hitler coalition into crypto-enemies of the Soviet Union, and virtual allies of Hitler.*

BODY-16   *The Soviet attitude toward this question assumed approximately its permanent form during 1942, when it must have seemed to the Soviet leaders that nothing but the crumbling defenses of Stalingrad stood between them and final disaster. It is understandable that in these desperate hours they were little disposed to appreciate Allied logistic problems and were bitter about the failure of the needed military relief to materialize.*

BODY-17   *Soviet postwar propaganda interpreted this event in such a way as to place Allied political motives and military capabilities in the worst possible light. It was stated that the Allies undertook the Normandy invasion only to forestall the inevitable single-handed triumph of the Soviet Union.*

BODY-18   *"To continue the war in the international situation which has arisen, and given the situation within Japan, would mean the destruction of the whole nation."*

BODY-19   *According to Max Beloff, in his book Soviet Policy in the Far -East, 1944-1951, the attribution of the Japanese collapse exclusively to Soviet victories in Manchuria remained a constant of Soviet comment on this subject from the end of the war on.*

BODY-20   *"Some faint signs of dissatisfaction with elements of the official line also appeared among military writers during the postwar period. This expressed itself not in any open opposition to the official line, but in indications that the professional military officers were experiencing tension between their direct experience of the military events of the war and the theoretical formulas in which they were required to express them."*

BODY-21   *"Our staffs never used such concepts as 'internal and external fronts'; they are useless since they do not explain the essence of the operational maneuver."*

BODY-22   *The very first words of the article were "The Munich capitulation," and this phrase was used regularly throughout. It was, moreover, devoid of the usual references to Marxist authorities. Although it carried a heavy scholarly apparatus, in a close text* of fifty pages, only two or three purely factual references to Soviet sources appeared.

BODY-23   "It was said that the book presented US foreign policy during the Second World War 'just as American imperialists themselves attempt to portray it.' This interpretation, it was said, conveyed the impression that the US government was opposed to the anti-Soviet policies of Churchill and the American imperialists, that it was a staunch friend of the Soviet Union throughout the struggle. Thus the book concealed the 'struggle within the anti-Hitler coalition' during the war, and ignored the 'fundamental opposition between the foreign policy of the USSR, on the one hand, and of the USA and Great Britain, on the other.'"

BODY-24   The most striking feature of their performance was the indisputable evidence it provided that the historians understood the nature of the capitulations they were forced to make.

BODY-25   "We are not inclined to grovel before the West," he said. "We carry our culture with dignity.... But to tear off the history of Russia from the history of other countries-- this would mean to return to a past which has been condemned, and it would hardly be right to start off on such a path."

BODY-26   "that the history of Soviet society is not history, but current politics."

BODY-27   "There were cases when the criticism of mistakes (recently made in the press, etc.) were met with hostility in the Institute."

BODY-28   The substance of Panferov's article was the complaint that the critics opposed any portrayal of the war which conveyed a true measure of the enormous sacrifices it had cost. In his article he described how he had questioned the generals during the last days of the war, and asked them to explain to him the nature of the victory that had been won. They could not answer, he said. Even they, the generals who had won the victory, were forced to admit that they did not fully understand the moral forces that had moved their armies. They stood before a puzzle, the sphinx of victories. Only the critics, sneered Panferov, the "crocks and potsherds," as he called them, were able to understand this great

BODY-29   "But, if you will, why minimize the strength of the enemy, his resourcefulness, his rapaciousness, his cunning, his military skill, his steadiness in battle, his ability to defend himself, to attack, and finally, to fight? Indeed, in depicting the enemy as a wooden head with eyes, we minimize the heroism of the Red Army. What kind of heroism is it to have beaten a wooden head with eyes? No, the enemy was strong, in his own way, able, cunning, and steady in battle."

BODY-30   The lasting significance of Panferov's article rests in the testament it gave of Russia's wartime experience. On the eve of the postwar campaign of falsifications and half-truths, which the regime hoped would blot out the unhappy memories of the war, one clear voice bore witness to the sufferings and sacrifices it had cost. It spoke not only for Panferov but for many of his colleagues as well, and indeed for the Russian people. Echoes of this testimony to the truth about the war were to be heard again in the postwar period.

BODY-31   "The field buzzed. And in this drone one could hear the agitation, the excitement caused by the recent shock, and, at the same time, the deep, sad weariness, the numbness, the half-sleep, that one observes in a crowded waiting room at night in a large railway junction."

BODY-32   "The attempt to poeticize that which is foreign to the life of the people, and foreign to poetry, has led to a false and crude ideological mistake."

BODY-33   "In the vigor and directness of its attack, Vershigora's article came close to matching the ardor of Panferov's polemic of two years before. The diary of Dzhigurda, which precipitated the dispute, was itself a patently honest portrayal of the thoughts, feelings, and behavior of people exposed to war. In simple, straightforward language, the author described the people around her, neither embellishing their virtues nor concealing their faults."

BODY-34   "It is not necessary to minimize the personal shortcomings of our people. But if one is to see the main, socialist thing above all, then the petty, personal shortcomings are not blown up disproportionately."

BODY-35   The almost complete absence of great literature on the worthy and necessary theme of the heroic defense of Leningrad convinces me that the aforementioned comrade is right. Crude facts (and they are always crude, particularly for those who have not had a whiff of them) cannot be written, and people are apparently still ashamed to write the prettified "little truths" which are always worse than open lies. And the result? The needed book about the great feat of Leningrad has not, and does not, come!

BODY-36   "The natural tendency of the Stalinist historical myths to disintegrate was accelerated by the problems which the new government faced. First, there was the succession itself: the new system of collective leadership had to be legitimized; the state administration, pulverized by Stalin, had to be reconstituted; long suppressed consumer demands had to be satisfied; a way out of the foreign policy impasse had to be found. Secondly, there were problems arising from the military-strategic situation created by the maturing of nuclear developments within the Soviet Union, and the continuing improvement of delivery capabilities in both world power blocs."

BODY-37   "the impact of the new strategic situation was reflected in Malenkov's efforts to damp down the sparks which might set off an international conflagration--which, in his words of 1954, would mean the 'destruction of world civilization.' The circumstances surrounding this declaration strongly suggest that Malenkov meant it as a powerful argument in defense of his policies."

BODY-38   "For the first time, the factor of surprise was accorded a significance which an age of nuclear weapons and transcontinental bombers made prudent and necessary."

BODY-39   "The main thesis presented was that fresh and original thought was needed to keep the Soviet military establishment responsive to the demands of contemporary military realities. It condemned the slavish attitude toward Stalin, which, it said, obtained among military writers. It asked scornfully why Stalin's thesis on the permanently operating factors should have been considered a new contribution to military science. 'Why was this permitted?'"

BODY-40   "It is necessary to put an end to this mistaken concept of the initial period of the war as quickly as possible, since in fact the operations of that period, in the main, had the character of withdrawal operations."

BODY-41   The Communist Party of the Soviet Union was the leading and directing force in the heroic struggle of the Soviet people against the German fascist aggressors, and raised outstanding commanders, who, headed by J. V. Stalin, demonstrated strategic and operational leadership....The fundamental creator of the victory over fascist Germany...was the Soviet people.

BODY-42   The fact that the Khrushchev faction, for tactical reasons in its struggle with Malenkov, had associated its program with Stalinist symbols left an opening for those who wished to declare their loyalty to Khrushchev to do so by resisting any revision of the war which had anti-Stalinist implications.

BODY-43   "A primitive interpretation of the initial period of the war, which distorts living reality, wherever it takes place -- in scientific works or in artistic works -- cannot be tolerated, since it distorts historical truth, and incorrectly orients our people, creating the impression that such precedents might, and even should, be repeated in the future."

BODY-44   Study and popularization of the history of the Great Patriotic War will help strengthen the Soviet people's military preparedness to crush any imperialist aggressor, and will help further to train the Soviet people in unshakable faith in the victory of their just cause, and in ardent Soviet patriotism and proletarian internationalism.

BODY-45   Strong tendencies toward the revaluation of the Stalinist historical legacy appeared even before the Twentieth Party Congress opened, and assumed a programmatic character at the conference of the readers of Questions of History, which was held at the end of January, 1956. Accurately anticipating the mood of the Congress which was to convene two weeks later, the conference outlined a revisionary program touching a broad range of established Soviet historical attitudes.

BODY-46   The Twentieth Party Congress encouraged this movement not only by giving it official auspices, but by supplying the substantive criticism of Stalin which served as the solvent of traditional historical attitudes. Khrushchev's secret speech, which portrayed Stalin as ignorant of military matters, and as criminally responsible for the initial unpreparedness of the Soviet Union and for subsequent defeats, was quickly made known to party members, and, indirectly, to the politically literate elements of the Soviet population. Beginning a few weeks after the adjournment of the Congress and continuing for several months thereafter, the Soviet press gave numerous signs of the shock impact which these revelations had had throughout the Soviet Union.

BODY-47   Included in this indictment was the charge, first made by Khrushchev in his secret speech, that the prewar 'industrial planning of the Soviet Union had not been properly geared to defense needs. Secondary points of the article ran a broad gamut' of criticism tending to deprecate, or even to debunk, the past official historiography of the war.

BODY-48   "The author could well say, in line with the spirit expressed in these criticisms, that there was 'the greatest historic importance in the fact that the Soviet socialist state gained allies among the majority of these capitalist states in the war against world fascism.'"

BODY-49   "After the Hungarian revolt, the anti-Stalin campaign, with its attendant revisionary impulses, was sharply curbed. Thereafter, little more was heard about the revision of the history of the war in the Soviet Union, until the subject was reopened, under more controlled conditions, toward the end of 1957."

BODY-50   "It must be said directly that this (the German attack) was not a surprise to the Supreme Soviet Military Command; many measures aimed at heightening the military preparedness and fighting capacity of the Soviet Armed Forces, at reorganizing them, were in the stage of being carried out and conducted at the time when fascist Germany attacked..."

BODY-51   "The most prominent feature of the new material was the blend of candor and caution it displayed in dealing with the initial period of the war. Acknowledgements of the failures of the first period were again made, but they were closely linked with arguments calculated to draw attention to the achievements."

BODY-52   "The attack of the German fascists on the Soviet Union was effected at a time when our Armed Forces were still in the process of reorganization and technical rearmament.... Courageously battling with the overwhelming forces of the adversary in the extremely unfavorable circumstances which arose in the initial period of war due to a whole number of causes and mistakes, they suffered heavy losses in personnel and fighting equipment, and were forced reluctantly to retreat into the interior of the country. In the face of the mortal danger hanging over our country, the Communist party aroused the whole Soviet people to a just defensive war against the fascist aggressors."

BODY-53   "It was characterized chiefly by a conservative concern to bolster the party's historical reputation, and to preserve intact the traditional image of Soviet wartime achievements. At the same time, it sought to retain the gains in historical objectivity achieved in 1955 and 1956. In other words, it encouraged a technically accurate account of the military history of the war, in a framework of political interpretations which removed the unfavorable reflections on the party itself."

BODY-54   "It is impermissible to underrate the rich experience gained in the waging of battles, much less to forget it. Despite the fact that a new weapon has appeared at the present time which, along with other factors, has had a great influence on our views regarding the conduct of battle operations in contemporary conditions, the experience of the Great Patriotic War has not lost its significance."

BODY-55   "The key event in stimulating a further development of the historiography of the war was a decision of the Central Committee in the fall of 1957 authorizing the Marxism-Leninism Institute to prepare a five-volume history of the war. P. N. Pospelov, a candidate member of the party presidium, with general responsibilities in ideological and propaganda matters, was named as the supervisor of the project. A new sector of the history of the Great Patriotic War was set up in the Marxism-Leninism Institute with a group of authors headed by Major General E. A. Boltin."

BODY-56   "The work is scheduled to be completed during the period 1960-1962. The Central Committee decree of autumn 1957, in addition to authorizing a textbook had the effect of focusing the attention and efforts of the whole military-historical community on the subject of the history of the war, and of starting something like a race to exploit the newly opened market."

BODY-57   "The wealth of detail which Platonov provides on this question presents a picture of stupidity and complacency on the Soviet side which is more damning than anything previously published in the Soviet Union and perhaps even outside the USSR."

BODY-58   He also assigns due weight to the variety of accidental factors which told in the final German failure to take Moscow. Unlike previous accounts which had reserved all credit in this event for Soviet staunchness and military skill, he speaks freely of German mistakes and difficulties. He points out, for example, that the quality of the German army had deteriorated badly by the time of the Moscow battle, with its infantry divisions reduced to half strength and its tank forces badly depleted. Moreover, in a startling admission for a Soviet author, he states correctly that the Germans "did not have winter uniforms, and that the equipment and a part of the infantry and artillery weapons were not adapted for use in winter conditions." (p. 248)

BODY-59   "In accordance with the situation which had arisen," he writes, "the military Council of the Western Front presented a plan for a counteroffensive of the front to General Headquarters on November 30." Platonov then notes the additions to the plan introduced over the next few days, and concluded: "Thus, the plan for the counteroffensive under Moscow was the result of the great creative activity of the front commands, the General Staff, and the Headquarters of the Supreme Command."

BODY-60 "The story of alleged Allied duplicity before and during the war is recounted by Platonov much as it has always been told in the Soviet Union. The Allies are depicted as having sought to buy their own security before the war by encouraging Germany to attack the Soviet Union."

BODY-61 "It is completely obvious that this was a recompense to Hitler for his undertaking to begin war against the Soviet Union."

missing pages 56-60

28 October 1959

OCI No. 5321/59
Copy No.

CURRENT INTELLIGENCE STAFF STUDY

THE SOVIET HISTORY OF WORLD WAR II
(Reference Title: Caesar X-59)

HR70-14
(U)

Office of Current Intelligence

CENTRAL INTELLIGENCE AGENCY

OCI No. 5321/59

SINO-SOVIET BLOC AREA
OFFICE OF CURRENT INTELLIGENCE
Reference Title:. CAESAR X-59

CURRENT INTELLIGENCE STAFF STUDY

The Soviet History of World War II

This is a working paper, the second to be published by the Sino-Soviet Studies Group, a merger of the CAESAR, POLO and ESAU projects. The group would welcome either written or oral comment on this paper, addressed to

THE SOVIET HISTORY OF WORLD WAR II

This paper seeks to answer questions posed by the recent increased attention to the history of the war in the Soviet Union. Why is the regime now encouraging historical writing on the war? What interpretations are being promoted? What are the political and military implications?

This is essentially a fact-finding study. Despite the importance of the war in Soviet history, and the politically sensitive nature of this topic in the Soviet Union, Soviet writing on the war has not been systematically examined in the West, and in general it has not been of such immediate political significance as to attract the continuing attention of intelligence. This gap defines the scope of the present study.

The paper identifies the issues which postwar propaganda created in this field and traces the evolution of Soviet views on these issues from the immediate postwar period to the present.

SUMMARY AND CONCLUSIONS

Until recent years, the Soviet leadership was consistent in regarding the history of the war as an instrument for influencing social attitudes rather than as a subject deserving truthful evaluation in its own right. Before and after Stalin, the Soviet official interpretation of the war reflected the current policies of the regime.

The Stalinist interpretation of the war was devised to conceal the traces of the wartime drift of the Soviet Union from its historical course of development, and to convince the Soviet people that nothing had intervened which would justify a change in past policies. Thus the history of the war became a paean to Stalin's political and military genius, a testament to the wisdom of party policies, an indictment of the perfidy of the capitalist world, a proof of the soundness of the Soviet system. The Stalinist version of the war distorted the historical facts in at least four major respects:

It presented the catastrophic defeats of the first year of the war as a preplanned and skillfully executed maneuver designed to set the conditions for a successful counteroffensive.

It magnified the roles of Stalin and the party in the achievement of victory, and diminished the roles of the military leaders and the ordinary people.

It depreciated the contributions of the Allies, and sought to transform their image in the public mind from partners in the anti-Hitler coalition into crypto-enemies of the Soviet Union and virtual allies of Hitler.

It claimed that the Soviet declaration of war and the defeat of the Kwantung army, rather than American military successes, had played the decisive role in bringing about the defeat of Japan.

Varying degrees of resistance to the imposition of this version of the war were manifested by those elements of the Soviet population most directly affected by it--the military, the historians, and the writers. Military officers indicated disdain for the concepts developed to idealize the military events of the war. Historians demonstrated inertial resistance to the postwar propaganda assault on the West and its attendant distortions of the Allied role in the war, and before succumbing to official pressure indicated their distaste for the political considerations which motivated it. The writers demonstrated outspoken opposition to the official line.

The reactions of all three groups were based not on political opposition to the regime, but on the inherent conflict between propaganda demands and their own professional standards. A marked tendency of the professional military was a preference for facts over theory, an attitude which seemed to reflect a concern that the excessive idealization of military events would prevent a proper evaluation and application of the lessons inherent in them. The historians appeared to feel that historical questions ought to be settled by historical rather than political criteria, and by the historians themselves. Writers who remained true to their art were unwilling, and in any case unable, to present what they conceived to be the epic of the war in the shallow terms of a political tract.

After Stalin's death, the official interpretation of the war underwent important changes. These changes reflected the Soviet leaders' apprehension that the Soviet people and the Soviet military establishment were being poorly prepared, by the unrealistic portrayal of the last war, for the kind of war which they now foresaw as possible. The Stalinist line, they felt, encouraged the dangerous illusion that war was easy, and it conditioned military officers to feel that retreats and slow attritional methods were normal means of conducting war. The main content of the new version of the war which emerged from these considerations in 1955 was that the early period of the war had been a defeat for the Soviet army, rather than a prelude to victory.

As the Twentieth Party Congress approached, new tendencies toward a break with the past appeared, giving fresh impetus to this reconsideration of the history of the war. The central feature of the new movement was the break with Stalin which was dramatized at the Congress. Khrushchev's secret speech, which portrayed Stalin as ignorant of military matters and as criminally responsible for the initial unpreparedness of the Soviet Union, cleared the way for removing the many distortions of history which derived from exaggeration of Stalin's role in the war. The early defeats of the Soviet army were interpreted now as due not only to the surprise of the German attack, as had been emphasized in 1955, but to the negligence of Stalin in failing to take the precautionary measures which elementary prudence and ample intelligence warnings had indicated were necessary. A more generous appraisal

- ii -

of the role of the Allies in the war was also fostered at this time.

After the Twentieth Party Congress, the need to halt the deterioration of political authority resulting from the anti-Stalin campaign threatened to halt also the progress toward honest military history. In the latter part of 1956, and in 1957, the party faced the choice of curtailing the revisionary historiography of the war to protect its immediate political interests, or of sustaining this historiography to encourage the professionalism and realism of military thought which it expressed and nourished.

Over the past year or more, Soviet policy in this sphere has been carefully calculated. It has sought to retain the gains in historical objectivity achieved in 1955 and 1956, but not at the cost of reflecting unfavorably on the party itself. The formula has been: to admit Soviet reverses in the early days of the war, but to emphasize Soviet achievements--and the party's leading role--in recovering from those reverses. The formula has also minimized the contribution of the USSR's allies to the victory.

The evolution of the historiography of the war toward a more accurate appraisal of military realities is of some importance, as in this area the regime has gradually accepted the concept of the utility of truth. This victory for the truth is a limited one, as the truth is surrounded by political propaganda with which the party justifies itself and its policies. Nevertheless, this development illustrates a tendency which has appeared in other areas of Soviet activity as well, and this tendency is likely to grow.

I. THE HISTORICAL ISSUES AND THE POSTWAR INTERPRETATION

The Initial Period of the Soviet German War

The most critical issue in the Soviet historiography of the war was the interpretation of the great defeats suffered by the Soviet army during the first period of the war. The immense material losses and incalculable human sufferings which the collapse of Soviet defenses entailed would have been embarrassing for any government to explain, but for a regime which staked its authority on its claim to foresee the future they were catastrophic in their implications. Soviet postwar propaganda sought to smother these implications by denying that any real defeats had taken place.

The first problem for Soviet propaganda was to explain the Soviet failure to anticipate and prepare for the initial German assault. There is ample evidence that the Soviet government was fully informed of the German intention to attack well before the invasion took place. Churchill has described the careful personal efforts he made to bring the seriousness of the situation to Stalin's attention. He has also told of other warnings conveyed to the Soviet government by subordinate British officials and the American government. Investigations of Soviet spy networks in Austria and Japan after the war revealed that Soviet intelligence had also uncovered advance information on the German invasion plans. Finally, Khrushchev in his secret speech to the Twentieth Party Congress cited many additional indications that had been made available to the Soviet government through its own diplomatic and military sources.

Soviet postwar propaganda made no acknowledgment of these advance warnings of the German intention to attack. Instead, it sought to turn to advantage the blunder which the Soviet government had committed in discounting these warnings. It depicted the Soviet Union as the victim of German "perfidy," it stressed the "suddenness" of the German attack. The initial defeats were presented as flowing from the natural disadvantage suffered by a peace-loving state in the face of a ruthless aggressor. At the same time, the pre-war policies of the Soviet Union, its industrialization programs, and its diplomatic and military encroachments in eastern Europe, were presented as calculated against an eventual German attack, and thus as responsible for the country's ability to withstand the shock when the attack came.

- 1 -

Secondly, Soviet propaganda had to explain the continuous defeats of the Soviet army during 1941, and the abandonment of huge territories and much of the population of the Baltic republics, Leningrad province, Byelorussia, and the Ukraine. In the light of these results, it was obvious that the Soviet army had not shown to advantage during the first months of the war. The operational command, which at that time was in the hands of the political marshals, Voroshilov, Timoshenko, and Budennyy, on the Northwestern, Western, and Southwestern fronts respectively, showed little capacity to cope with the mobile conditions of warfare created by deep German penetrations of prepared defense positions. Deprived of large mobile reserves and air support, and bound by the Supreme Command strategy of defending "each inch of native soil," the army repeatedly permitted large forces to be encircled where a more flexible strategy might have saved them. To mention only the largest operations, approximately a half-million men, according to German figures, were lost in each of the huge encirclements around Kiev and Vyazma.

In explaining these disasters, Soviet propaganda sought to have it both ways--to enhance the dimensions of the final Soviet achievement in stopping the German offensive, while minimizing the mistakes which made great achievements necessary. It was acknowledged that a "difficult situation" had been created, that a "mortal danger hung over the Soviet country," and yet a picture was presented of the Soviet Supreme Command as being in masterly control of the situation at all times, and as influencing the course of events toward its final successful consummation. The strategy of the Supreme Command, it was said, was to give space for time, and by "exhausting and bleeding white the enemy," to prepare the grounds for a counteroffensive.

There were two formulas in Soviet postwar propaganda which were very important in the official account of this period, and which express the whole tenor of this account. The first was the so-called strategy of "active defense," which was represented as a Supreme Command plan embracing not only the tactical methods of aggressive counteraction in defense, but the whole strategic conception of the early

- 2 -

period of Soviet operations.* The second and more important formula was the so-called strategic "counteroffensive," which also was said to embrace, as parts of a preconceived plan, the whole complex of defensive actions conducted by the Soviet army preliminary to the launching of the actual counteroffensive.* The effect of both formulas, of course, was to embellish the reputation of the Soviet leadership by presenting the early defeats as necessary preliminary stages to the ultimate victory.

Finally, Soviet propaganda had to interpret the ultimate stopping of the German advance and the saving of Moscow. The facts concerning these events were as follows. The German armies on the central front, after rapid initial progress, reached the vicinity of Smolensk by mid-July, 1941. Here the advance on Moscow paused, not only because of Russian resistance, but because of cross purposes in the German High Command. Hitler wished to divert the tank armies from the Moscow

---

* The term "active defense" had two meanings. Its first meaning, which it generally carried in the writings of the wartime period, expressed the idea that the defensive actions of the Soviet troops were designed not only to stop the enemy, but to keep up the morale of the Soviet troops themselves, to "temper their regiments" for a subsequent transition to offensive action. This meaning derived from Stalin's Order of the Day No. 308, of September 18, 1941, which created the first guards units. Its second meaning, which it assumed in postwar propaganda, expressed the idea that the defensive actions of the Soviet troops were preplanned to hold back the progress of the enemy until the permanently operating factors of war could be brought into play. The direct source of the postwar flourishing of this concept was Stalin's electoral speech of February 9, 1946.

** The doctrine of the "counteroffensive" was first publicized in Stalin's letter to Colonel Razin of February, 1947. Stalin derived the ideas expressed in this letter from an article entitled "The Strategic Counteroffensive," by Major General N. Talenskiy, which was published in Military Thought, No. 6, 1946.

- 3 -

direction to assist in the flank attacks on Leningrad and Kiev, while the German generals wished to continue the advance on the central front. While the generals vainly temporized, and in the end acquiesced to Hitler's decision, many weeks of the best campaigning weather were allowed to fritter away. Finally, on 2 October, the advance on Moscow was resumed, but by the time the first successes around Vyazma had been consolidated the fall slush had set in. Slowed to a crawl by the weather and the stiffening Russian resistance, the advance finally petered out a few miles from Moscow, and was then mauled back by the Soviet counteroffensive which began on 6 December.

The reasons for the failure of the German offensive are many, and in large part of German origin. An important factor has been mentioned, the conflicts between Hitler and the generals, which in turn reflected the excessiveness of the demands which Hitler had imposed upon his forces. By the time of the final German advance on Moscow, German forces were overextended, both in terms of logistic communications and in the ratio of operational reserves to committed forces. Men and machines were exhausted from the long summer campaigns and the shifting of armies from one front to another over a great territorial expanse. German divisions had been thinned out before the beginning of the Russian campaign to spread the available manpower and armor among the 146 divisions which participated in the invasion. While they may have enjoyed a brief relative superiority during the early period of the war after the initial surrenders of Soviet troops, this was certainly lost by the end of the year. Finally, the cold weather which came on early and rapidly in 1941 caught the Germans unprepared, since in anticipation of a lightning victory they had not provided winter clothing for the troops.

Soviet postwar propaganda discounted all these accidental factors as having played any effective role in the final outcome. German logistic problems and leadership conflicts, while mentioned occasionally in general disparagements of German strategy and military science, were never admitted as decisive factors. The weather was mentioned in Soviet accounts, but only as interfering with Soviet operations. The manpower relationship was always claimed to be in the German favor, and the number of 170 German and 38 satellite divisions attributed to the German invasion force by the Russians during the war was retained in subsequent accounts. In short, any factor which tended to reduce the credit due the Soviet leadership and armed forces for stopping the German invasion was ignored in Soviet postwar propaganda.

- 4 -

Credits for the Victory

The broadest issue raised by the Soviet historiography of the war was the explanation of the final victory. In its most important aspect, this involved the question of which the four pillars of Soviet wartime society--the army, the party, the people, or Stalin alone--deserved the laurels of victory, and hence the rewards and prerogatives which they symbolized. It will be seen that this question cut across all others, and became the principal political issue of the Soviet interpretation of the war.

In considering the merits of the claims that could be advanced for the several aspirants, and the way in which the credits were in fact alloted, it will be logical to start with Stalin, since his figure loomed largest in Soviet post-war accounts.

Just what Stalin's role was in the strategic direction of the Soviet army is not entirely clear. Khrushchev's account in his secret speech of the telephone calls he had made to Vasilevskiy and Malenkov at the time of the Kharkov battle suggests that Stalin exercised at least a general supervision over military operations. It is probable that his dictatorial habits and affectations of military competence led him to interfere more directly in military matters than the other Allied leaders commonly permitted themselves to do. But in the actual conception and direction of military operations he was probably cautious enough to limit his interference to the confirmation or veto of plans presented by General Headquarters. Even within these limits, and judging by the bits of evidence available, his record as a war leader was far from consistently good. His gross error in discounting the numerous intelligence indications of the German preparations for attack has been mentioned above. His strategy of "no retreat" during the first period of the war played into the hands of the German encircle-ment tactics, and his stubborn insistence on continuing the Kharkov offensive in 1942 after the Soviet position had become hopeless was, to say the least, militarily unjustified. His competence for command was apparently also negatively affected by his moodiness of character. Khrushchev charged that Stalin became panic-stricken in 1941, and Churchill's account of Stalin's desperate appeal for a British expeditionary corps at that time lends corroboration to this charge.

- 5 -

In postwar propaganda, however, Stalin was transformed into the "greatest commander of all the ages." All military operations were said to have been carried out according to his plans and under his immediate direction. He was said to have "worked out anew" and, for the first time in history, applied with full effect the "strategic counteroffensive," which constituted the greatest contribution in the annals of military science.

The army suffered most directly from the postwar inflation of the Stalin image. The record of the professional military leaders during the war was good. Whatever their merits when compared with their opposite numbers in the West, and there are differences of opinion on this score, they were the men who stood at the head of the troops when victory was achieved. Moreover, their contribution was dramatic. It was after Zhukov took over from the old Bolshevik Timoshenko, as Commander-in-Chief of the Western Front, that Moscow was saved and the first Soviet counteroffensive successfully carried out. It was also after Zhukov took over as overall commander of the southern fronts, and after the commissar system had been abolished in the army, that Stalingrad was saved, and the series of operations launched that led to ultimate victory. The figure of Zhukov in these key events of the war was symbolic of the professional military's role in rescuing the regime from the consequences of its own incompetence.

In postwar propaganda, the marshals rapidly faded into the background. Zhukov's fall from honor has often been noted. It was so swift and complete that the Soviet press observed the first anniversary of the fall of Berlin without mentioning his name. No other military figure was named in Pravda on that day either, nor on the other major anniversaries of the next few years. The articles published on the occasion of Stalin's seventieth birthday, in 1949, performed the equally remarkable feat of reviewing the whole course of the war without naming a single Soviet general officer.

The party's role in the war is perhaps the most difficult to evaluate because it was so closely woven into the fabric of Soviet society that it is hard now to distinguish, through the smokescreen of propaganda raised on its behalf, where party inspiration left off, and public initiative began in the great social and military achievements of the war. Unquestionably, the party's traditional role as the leader and coordinator of national energies was diminished during the war, as increasing reliance came to be placed on nonparty channels of public control, and as extraordinary

- 6 -

governmental and military bodies arose to take over direction of the war effort. To name merely the activity which the party later most vigorously claimed for its own credit, the partisan movement, the facts seem to be that the party had little to do with organizing the movement, and established control later only partially and with difficulty. In general, the conclusion seems safe that among the instruments available to the Soviet leadership for conducting the war effort the party apparatus performed an auxiliary function.

Thus it is understandable why, when the leadership decided after the war to return to the course of development that the war had interrupted, an important element in that reaction was the reassertion of the party's traditional place in Soviet life. This necessarily involved a recasting of the history of the war to show the party's role in a more befitting light. A very important feature of the postwar history was the claim that the party had "always and everywhere" inspired and led the people's resistance to the Germans. This claim was advanced particularly, but by no means exclusively, with respect to the civilian aspects of the wartime achievements--the evacuation of industry to the east, the feats of labor heroism performed at the rear, the partisan war carried on behind enemy lines. As Pravda put it, in criticizing Fadeyev's The Young Guard, in 1947: "The party everywhere and always introduced an organizing basis. Communists did not for a minute lose the leading role."

Finally, it is necessary to mention the role of the people in the war. Their contribution had been so massive, and so clearly affirmed by the regime during the war, that it stood in the way of any other claimant for exclusive honors. If this record were allowed to stand, the regime's own claims to indispensability, based on the supposed political immaturity of the masses, might well be open to question. Thus, a fact which would be taken for granted under any other regime--that the war had been won by the sacrifices and achievements of the people--in Soviet conditions became inadmissible. In Soviet postwar propaganda, the record of the people's role in the war was not openly contested, it was simply displaced.

The Role of the Allies

The role of the Allies in the war posed a particularly embarrassing problem for Soviet postwar propaganda, since any acknowledgment of the real contributions the Allies had made would tend to invalidate the image of a corrupt and hostile West which it was seeking to create. The task of Soviet

propaganda, thus, was to blot out as far as possible the
friendly memories of the wartime alliance, by besmirching
the motives for which the allied states fought, and by dis-
paraging their achievements.

The response of the Western Allies to Russia's plight
in 1941 was prompt and generous, and the material and military
contribution which the West made to the final victory was very
great. Allied material aid was extended at a time, and under conditions, which imposed a very real sacrifice on the
Allies' own war effort. In addition, as the war progressed,
the Allies brought to bear a military pressure on Germany
which contributed materially to speeding the collapse of the
German war machine.

According to American sources, the value of American
Lend-Lease shipments to Russia during the war totaled over
$11,000,000,000. British shipments and American private re-
lief added considerably to this total. Walter Kerr, in his
book The Russian Army, presents additional figures which bring
out in a graphic way the significance of this aid to the Soviet army. During the first year of deliveries alone, he says,
Washington and London shipped to Russia 3,052 planes, 4,084
tanks, 30,031 vehicles, and 831,000 tons of miscellaneous supplies, of which the major part got through. As Kerr points
out, the relative value of these figures can be grasped if
they are compared with the numbers of 1,136 planes and 2,091
tanks which, according to Russian claims, the Germans lost
during 52 days of the heaviest fighting in the first year of
the war. There are many indications from Russian sources, too,
of the value they placed on this aid during the war. Stalin's
anger at delays in the arrival of American equipment was indicative in this connection. The impress which Allied aid
made on the Soviet population, indications of which are scat-
tered throughout Soviet literature, is another sign of its
scope and significance. Even the language has recorded the
dimensions of American wartime aid in its transformation of
the name "Willys" into a Russian household word.

As for the rest, the Allied military role in the war, the
story is familiar enough to need no detail here. Beginning in
Africa, in 1942, the Allies began to build up a steadily mount-
ing pressure on Germany which engaged and wasted the dwindl-
ing resources which were desperately needed on the eastern
front. Soviet propaganda made much of the claim later that
no German units were withdrawn from the eastern front as a result of Allied operations (in fact, at least two SS divisions
were withdrawn to meet the Normandy invasion), but this is

- 8 -

beside the point. The real contribution of the Allies was
measured not in the juggling of German divisions which it
produced, but in the German energies absorbed by a series of
Allied second fronts, in Africa, Sicily, Italy, and France.

Soviet postwar propaganda was not content merely to
minimize the Allied role in the war, but sought actively to
transform the image of the Allies from partners in the anti-
Hitler coalition into crypto-enemies of the Soviet Union,
and virtual allies of Hitler. The principal device used to
achieve this end was to hammer home the accusation that the
real aim of Western policy before the war had been to iso-
late the USSR, and, in the final account, to embroil it in
war with Germany.

In its broadest application this charge affected the
Soviet official interpretation of the whole prewar period.
Beginning with the Paris Peace Conference, at which it was
asserted the "Russian question" occupied the primary place,
almost every major event of European diplomacy affecting the
USSR was made to fit into this framework. The Dawes Plan
which loosed a "golden rain of American dollars" into German war industry, the Four Power Pact which signified Anglo-
French willingness to come to terms with fascism, the Polish-
German nonaggression pact of 1934 which set a precedent for
replacing the principle of collective security by a system of
bilateral pacts, the Anglo-German naval agreement of 1935
which proclaimed Britain's disavowal of the principle of re-
stricting German remilitarization--were all seen in the Soviet account as stages in the consistent Western policy of
isolating the USSR and encouraging German aggression.

The major event affected by this line of interpretation
was, of course, the Munich agreement. The facts surrounding
this episode were such as to lend themselves to almost any
indictment of the strategy and morality of Western policy that
the Soviet Union would wish to make. The agreement was in
fact strategically defective in that it excluded the Soviet
Union from the joint action of the directing nations, and
morally defective in that it legalized violence. But these
indictments, recognized as valid in Western literature, were
not broad enough for the purposes of Soviet postwar propaganda. Instead, Stalin's phrase of 1939, that the Munich
agreement was the "price of an undertaking (by Germany) to
launch war on the Soviet Union" was resurrected as the basis
of the Soviet historical interpretation. The Western leaders were portrayed as active plotters with Hitler for war. In

- 9 -

Soviet postwar historiography the word "deal" (sgovor) became the official cachet of Munich, and historians who had seen in the Western behavior at Munich simply a concession or capitulation to Nazi threats were made to see their error.

A second issue for Soviet postwar propaganda on the Allied role in the war was the matter of Allied material aid. For Soviet postwar propaganda, any acknowledgment of the magnitude and usefulness of this aid could serve no political purpose, as it would document the indebtedness of the Soviet Union to a foreign state, which the Soviet Union would be loath to admit in any event, and least of all to the "bulwark of world capitalism." Moreover, it would diminish to some degree the luster of the Soviet Union's own industrial achievements, which were claimed to rest on the far-sighted industrialization programs carried out by the regime during the first five year plans. Thus, the matter of Allied supplies was mentioned very sparingly in Soviet postwar accounts of the war, and where mentioned was always presented as an exchange for Soviet raw materials, or as a paltry recompense for the Russian contributions of blood and time.

The most publicized of the issues affecting the Allied role in the war was the question of the second front. The Soviet attitude toward this question assumed approximately its permanent form during 1942, when it must have seemed to the Soviet leaders that nothing but the crumbling defenses of Stalingrad stood between them and final disaster. It is understandable that in these desperate hours they were little disposed to appreciate Allied logistic problems and were bitter about the failure of the needed military relief to materialize. But even after the passions of the moment cooled, the second front issue apparently appeared to the Soviet leaders as too useful a device to abandon. During the war it contributed a certain psychological leverage to the Soviet Union in dealings with the Allies, and probably went a long way toward cancelling out whatever sense of indebtedness the Allied supplies may have carried with them. After the war, it served as a prop for the claim that the Soviet Union had borne the brunt of the struggle against Hitler.

The basis of the Soviet postwar charge that the Allies had shown bad faith in this matter was the joint communiqué published in London and Washington after the Molotov visit in the spring of 1942. The communiqué said in part that "in the course of the conversations full understanding was reached with regard to the urgent task of creating a second front in Europe in 1942." Churchill has explained that the purpose of

- 10 -

the communiqué was to make the Germans apprehensive and hold as many of their troops in the west as possible. So as not to mislead the Russians, he took care to give Molotov an aide memoire, stating that he could "give no promise in the matter." In postwar comment on the subject, Soviet propaganda ignored the aide memoire. Instead, it bent every effort to show that the Allies had gone back on their word, and had done so, moreover, with the deliberate aim of dragging out the war and exhausting the Russians.

A fourth issue was the Normandy invasion. Soviet postwar propaganda interpreted this event in such a way as to place Allied political motives and military capabilities in the worst possible light. It was stated that the Allies undertook the Normandy invasion only to forestall the inevitable single-handed triumph of the Soviet Union. Moreover, it was charged that the Allies deliberately delayed their breakout from the Normandy beachhead for two and a half months, while watching developments on the Soviet-German front, and playing with the possibility of a compromise peace. In all of this, Soviet postwar propaganda placed great stress on the alleged inconsequential resistance put up by the Germans to the Allied invasion. It was claimed that the German divisions in Europe were not of first combat quality. During the whole period of the Normandy invasion, according to the Soviet postwar propaganda account, not a single German division was transferred from the Soviet front. Consequently, no significance could be attached to the Normandy invasion as easing the situation in any substantial degree on the eastern front.

A highly derogatory appraisal of Allied military capabilities was also given in connection with the Ardennes battle and the final advance through Germany. The former was presented as a major collapse of the Allied military position which would have been fatal had not Stalin, in response to Churchill's urgent plea, advanced the date of the Soviet winter offensive, and thus forced the Germans to abandon their attack and withdraw their forces to the eastern front. The final Allied advance through Germany was also explained as the result of the German political decision to concentrate all forces against the Russians and to leave the way open for the Allies to reach Berlin first.

The Pacific War

The principal issue raised by the Soviet account of the Pacific War was the interpretation of the Japanese surrender. The Soviet Union from the beginning maintained that it was the

- 11 -

Soviet declaration of war and the defeat of the Kwantung army, rather than the atomic bomb, which forced the Japanese to capitulate. The Soviet argument was based principally on three assertions: (1) that the Allies had achieved no significant military successes against the Japanese during the course of the Pacific War, (2) that the main military strength of Japan remained throughout the war untouched in Manchuria, and (3) that in 1945 Japan was still capable of continuing the war for another two years at least. This latter assertion was based on American military estimates, made in 1944, and 1945, of the requirements for the invasion of the Japanese home islands.

The role of the atomic bomb was usually ignored, or summarily dismissed, in Soviet accounts of the Japanese surrender. The most circumstantial Soviet argument on this point was offered by V. Avarin in his second book on the Pacific war, published in 1952. It was based on the data presented in the United States Strategic Bombing Survey regarding the deliberations in the Japanese Government during the last days before the decision to surrender was taken. Part of Avarin's argument was based on the timing of these events. The atomic bomb, he observed, was dropped on 6 August, and resulted in no particular reaction in Japanese official circles. The Soviet declaration of war reached Tokyo on the morning of 9 August, and was followed by a frantic series of official meetings, concluding with the Imperial Conference in the night of 9-10 August. Part of his argument was based also on the substance of the discussions. The key element here was the statement of the emperor announcing his decision to accept surrender. In it, he did not mention the atomic bomb, but said in part (according to Avarin's translation): "To continue the war in the international situation which has arisen, and given the situation within Japan, would mean the destruction of the whole nation."* This, according to Avarin, proved that the point at issue was "not the atomic bomb or strategic bombing, but 'the international situation which had arisen,' i.e., the entrance of the Soviet Union into the war against Japan. . . ."

---

* The emperor's words as given in the Strategic Bombing Survey are as follows: "Thinking about the world situation and the internal Japanese situation, to continue the war means nothing but the destruction of the whole nation;" Avarin obviously shaded his translation to support his argument.

- 12 -

Unlike many of the other issues discussed in this chap-
ter, there was very little development or change in the Soviet
interpretation of the Japanese surrender during the postwar
period. According to Max Beloff, in his book Soviet Policy in
the Far East, 1944-1951, the attribution of the Japanese collapse exclusively to Soviet victories in Manchuria remained
a constant of Soviet comment on this subject from the end of
the war on. All the major elements of this account were
present in the earliest analyses of this event noted. Colonel
M. Tolchenov, a prominent military writer, set out the main
lines of this argument in 1945, although in somewhat less
categorical terms than later became customary. He cited
Allied military estimates as proof that Japan was still capable of resistance at the end, and claimed that most foreign
newspapers recognized that Soviet intervention was "one of
the decisive factors" compelling the enemy to lay down his
arms. An accompanying article assessed the significance of
the atomic bomb, expressing some cautious optimism as to its
future peacetime implications, but concluding that it was ir-
relevant to the final outcome of the Pacific War and invoking
the authority of Generals Arnold and Chennault in support of
this conclusion.

II. INTERNAL RESISTANCE TO THE POSTWAR LINE ON THE WAR

During its development in the postwar period, the Soviet official interpretation of the war evoked varying degrees of resistance from elements of the population most directly affected--the professional military, the historians, and the writers.

The Professional Military

Although military writers played a key role in developing the official version of the war, they did not abdicate their professional integrity entirely to propaganda criteria, and, in their wartime writings at least, provided snatches of direct testimony on the real nature of wartime events. Some faint signs of dissatisfaction with elements of the official line also appeared among military writers during the postwar period. This expressed itself not in any open opposition to the official line, but in indications that the professional military officers were experiencing tension between their direct experience of the military events of the war and the theoretical formulas in which they were required to express them.

In the summer of 1945, a small unsigned article in Military Thought, the theoretical organ of the General Staff, first drew attention to this latter phenomenon. It took to task a number of specialized military journals for exaggerating the roles of their own services in the war, and for neglecting the Soviet doctrine on the coordinated action of all arms. These journals, said the article, "raise the basic question of the military employment of their own forces in combined arms battle poorly or not at all, and sometimes, in interpreting the experience of the military operations of their forces, attribute to them an independent significance." The Air Forces journal came in for particular criticism in this regard.

A more interesting case was a crusty article by Major General A. Penchevskiy, "Concerning Operations for Encirclement and Operational Terminology," in Military Thought, No. 6/7, 1945, which disputed the concept of "internal and external fronts" in an encirclement operation. This concept

- 14 -

OFFICIAL USE ONLY

BODY-20

was already becoming part of the legend of the Stalingrad operation, where, it was claimed, an "external front" had been formed on the encircling ring to prevent a breakin by Manstein's relief column, as well as an "internal front" to prevent a breakout by von Paulus' army. The use of this concept to buttress the claim that Stalin always beat the enemy "for sure," foreseeing on a large scale all the countermeasures that the enemy might possibly undertake, gave it a political significance. "In the planning of an operation," said Penchevskiy, "the forces and means of an army and front (fronts) are never under any circumstances divided between internal and external fronts (lines). They are divided according to operational objectives, and tasks are established by defined lines." He concluded with a blunt dismisal of the theory. "Our staffs never used such concepts as 'internal and external fronts'; they are useless since they do not explain the essence of the operational maneuver."

A still more interesting case was an article by General of the Army Eremenko, entitled "Counterblows in a Contemporary Defensive Operation," which appeared in Military Thought, No. 3, 1949. This was a notable article if for no other reason than that, at the height of the Stalin apotheosis, it mentioned Stalin only once, in the opening paragraph, and the adjective "Stalinist" once, in the last. Moreover, it dealt with the question of the counteroffensive in such a way as to obscure the role of the Supreme Commander in the direction of this operation and to enhance the role of army and front commanders. This resulted from the fact that Eremenko attributed to the counterblow (i.e., an operation of an army or front, larger than a counterattack, but smaller than a counteroffensive) the crucial role in triggering the counteroffensive, specifically with reference to Moscow and Kursk. He spoke of the counterblows in these two battles as "turning into" counteroffensives. This phraseology was, in itself, not unorthodox, but Eremenko made it appear that the army or front commander who made the decision for a counterblow was, in effect, the agent responsible for the counteroffensive. This, in the atmosphere of 1949, was perilously close to lese majesty.

There is evidence that the unorthodoxy of this article was the result not of careless writing but of blunt military honesty. Time and again, Eremenko missed the obvious opportunities to throw in a sop to Stalin's vanity. Repeatedly, he spoke of the counteroffensive as "growing out of," or "developing from," the counterblows launched by "our troops," without mentioning that it was "organized" by Stalin, as good propaganda practice required. In one place he went even further, and implicitly credited Zhukov with preparing the counteroffensive under Moscow.

The ideological lapses of this article were thrown into stronger relief by a vigorously orthodox article on the counteroffensive which Eremenko published two years later. It provided a whole catalogue of the standard formulas praising Stalin as the genius exponent of this strategy. The spirit of this article contrasted so sharply with the earlier one that the conclusion seems inescapable that considerations of political discretion had propmted it.

The Historians

The professional historians were blocked off from the military history of the war by political decisions taken at war's end, and thenceforth restricted themselves to the diplomatic history of the wartime period. In this field, a significant number of them displayed a relatively objective attitude toward the West up through 1947, and some beyond that date.

One work of considerable interest was the first volume of a series, Works on Modern and Contemporary Histroy, which was brought out by the History Institute in 1948. This volume was severely criticized later for many departures from ideological orthodoxy. One article in it, "The German-Fascist Drang nach Osten after Munich," by F. I. Notovich, is illustrative of the general scholarships and political detachment of the volume. The main criticism later directed against this article was that it described the Munich agreement as a "capitulation," rather than as a "deal" or "bargain." The very first words of the article were "The Munich capitulation," and this phrase was used regularly throughout. It was, moreover, devoid of the usual references to Marxist authorities. Although it carried a heavy scholarly apparatus, in a close text of fifty pages, only two or three purely factual references to Soviet sources appeared.

- 16 -

Another example of postwar unorthodoxy in Soviet historiography was a book published in 1947, by Professor G. Deborin, entitled "International Relations and the Foreign Policy of the USSR, 1917-1945," IV: The Years of the Great Patriotic War. This book was apparently withdrawn from circulation sometime in 1949, and is not now available. According to the Soviet press, the book was published by the Higher Diplomatic School as an informal student manual and enjoyed circulation in educational institutions in this capacity. Official attention was drawn to the book, apparently, when the contemporary history sector of the History Institute attempted to republish it under the seal of the Academy of Sciences.

The substantive criticism of the book was focused on its alleged pro-American bias. It was said that the book presented US foreign policy during the Second World War "just as American imperialists themselves attempt to portray it." This interpretation, it was said, conveyed the impression that the US government was opposed to the anti-Soviet policies of Churchill and the American imperialists, that it was a staunch friend of the Soviet Union throughout the struggle. Thus the book concealed the "struggle within the anti-Hitler coalition" during the war, and ignored the "fundamental opposition between the foreign policy of the USSR, on the one hand, and of the USA and Great Britain, on the other." On a more specific issue, the second front, the book also was said to have given a distorted interpretation. The Western delay in opening a second front was attributed to the inability of US and British leaders to evaluate the developing situation in 1942 correctly, to their overestimation of the Hitler forces. Thus, the prolonged delay in opening the second front was ascribed to "shortsighted" US and British leaders. Finally, the official critics hinted darkly at improper motives in the publication of the book.

As the critics were clear to point out, historians were held responsible not only for what they published, but also for what they said. A statement made in a classroom lecture will serve as a last illustration of the laggardness of the Soviet historical community in accepting the postwar official line on the war. The case in point was that of Professor Zvavich, a specialist on British history. The most startling of the words he was alleged to have uttered were described as follows:

In the lecture course given at the Higher Diplomatic School, Zvavich committed a direct falsification of history, asserting that a turning point in the course of the war took place as a result of the landing of the Americans in Italy. (Voprosy Istorii No. 2, 1949, 156)

The full fury of the ideological reaction fell on the historical community during the years 1948 and 1949, when, under the goad of the party press, a series of meetings was held to place one historian after another on the rack of public criticism for the edification of his fellows. The climax of this campaign came in the spring of 1949, when the second issue of Questions of History for that year was held up for five months, while a reorganization of the editorial board was effected. The resistance which the historians displayed was evoked not by clashes over particular issues, but by professional disdain for the political criteria which defined the party's demands. The most striking feature of their performance was the indisputable evidence it provided that the historians understood the nature of the capitulations they were forced to make.

There were signs, first of all, that the historians attempted to deflect, or blunt, or even to shield each other from the sharp edge of party criticism. The behavior of the editorial board of Questions of History itself was remarkable in this respect. It displayed tact and forebearance in the case of N. Rubinshteyn, for example, the author of a book on Russian historiography, and the first victim of the ideological reaction, by allowing him to initiate the discussion of his criticized book, rather than subjecting him to immediate attack by others. Its action in the case of I. I. Mints, a specialist in the early Soviet period, was even bolder. At a time when Mints had become the main target of the party attack, the editorial board allowed him to publish a lead article, in the first issue of 1949, which in effect constituted an apologia for the historical community. This article listed all the names of the leading Soviet historians, proclaimed their contributions to Soviet historical science, and (perhaps by a slip of the pen, becuase his article was otherwise very dutiful in this respect) attributed to his own colleagues, rather than to Stalin, the credit for laying the "basis for the study of the Soviet period of the history of our country."

- 18 -

In addition to Questions of History itself, individual historians also made efforts to stem the course of party reaction. At the beginning of the critical campaign, for example, there was at least one historian (K. Vazilevich) who stood openly against the basic chauvinist tendency of the official line. "We are not inclined to grovel before the West," he said. "We carry our culture with dignity.... But to tear off the history of Russia from the history of other countries--this would mean to return to a past which has been condemned, and it would hardly be right to start off on such a path." In the first discussion of Mints' book on the first years of the Soviet regime, it was reported that one speaker (A. I. Gukovskiy) attempted to impugn Mints' loyalty. The subsequent speakers, it was noted, "unanimously rejected" this insinuation. Again, in the discussion of Works on Modern and Contemporary History it was reported: "Attempts to soften the sharpness of the criticism appeared, for example, in the speech of A. Z. Manfred, who accompanied his adknowledgment of the mistaken character of Eggerts' article with ambiguous compliments regarding the author's "great skill,' 'ability to master the material,' etc."

Individual authors, not infrequently, showed considerable stubbornness in refusing to bow meekly to official criticism. I. M. Lemin, for example, the author of The Foreign Policy of Great Britain from Versailles to Locarno, was reported sticking to his guns at the end of the critical session on his book.

It is necessary to note, at the same time, the unserious and irresponsible attitude which the author of the book himself displayed toward the discussion. Admitting, in general terms, that certainly "there are many shortcomings in the book," that "there are certain bad sounding words," and that "the tone is inappropriate in a number of cases," I. M. Lemin at the same time attempted, without any proof, to deny all the concrete and argued complaints and observations about the book made by the speakers. As a result of the false position taken by him, I. M. Lemin in fact rejected the critical review of his book, in the light of the criticism to which it was subjected at the discussion, and his concluding words failed completely to satisfy those present. (Voprosy Istorii, No. 6, 1948, 139)

- 19 -

The occasional cynical remarks which some historians
made during these critical sessions revealed, more eloquent-
ly than any disquistion, their full awareness of the purely
political considerations which motivated the official reaction. Professor Lutskiy, for example, in attempting to ward
off attacks on his sector of the History Institute, referred
to the opinion which, he said, was commonly held in historical
circles, "that the history of Soviet society is not history,
but current politics." A similar theme in the defensive remarks of the criticized historians was the complaint that
they had been victimized by the swift change in the official
line after the war.

F. I. Notovich, for example, the author of the article
on German post-Munich policy, considered above, used this
defense.

> Still more unsatisfactory was the speech of F. I.
> Notovich, who at first refused to recognize any
> substantial mistakes at all in his understanding
> or evaluation of the Munich policy in his article.
> Only in his second speech, which followed the deci-
> sive criticism of his first, did Comrade Notovich
> acknowledge that he had permitted "false notes" in
> it, and that his article did not correspond to the
> demands of militant party historical science. How-
> ever, even in his second speech, F. I. Notovich in-
> sinuated false notes. He explained the errors of
> his article not as arising from a misunderstanding
> of the essence of the Munich agreement, but as a re-
> sult of the fact that he had "printed in 1948 an ar-
> ticle written in 1945...." (Voprosy Istorii, No. 12, 1948, 177.)

Perhaps more significant than these displays of individual courage or stubbornness were the signs (naturally heavily
veiled in Soviet sources) of something like an organized resistance by the historical community to the party's ideological campaign. This appeared most clearly in the virtual
boycott of the discussion of Rubinshteyn's text book held
by the Ministry of Higher Education, in March, 1948. Of
the speakers reported at the meeting, only three appeared
to be historians of importance (S. A. Pokrovskiy, A. L.
Sidorov, and Ye. N. Gorodetskiy), the others being mainly
docents, or professors from outside Moscow. The abstention
of the first-rate historical figures from the meeting was

all the more striking in view of the high sponsorship of the affair, and the importance which the authorities obviously attached to it. Both Sidorov and Gorodetskiy, at the meeting, referred to the absence of the major professors in terms which suggested that a "feat of silence" was being performed, Complaining that the initiative for the criticism had come from outside the historical community, Sidorov stated: "Even now, at this present conference, the majority of the members of the department (of Moscow State University) are absent.... A certain inwardness on the part of these institutions (the History Institute, and the Academy of Social Sciences), and the absence of prominent historians at the present meeting, characterizes, to a significant degree, the general position on the historical front...." Gorodetskiy referred sarcastically to the "absence of the so-called pillars of historical science from the discussion...." Later, on several occasions, it was implied that this abstention of the Moscow historical community from the meeting had been a deliberate act.

Later criticism revealed other cases of group opposition to the party's ideological campaign. A lead article in Questions of History, at the end of 1948, for example, asserted: "There were cases when the criticism of mistakes (recently made in the press, etc.) were met with hostility in the Institute." Also: "The Institute did not organize work on the exposure of foreign bourgeois historiography, and did not conduct an attack on foreign falsifiers of history. This work, until recently, has been considered in the Institute as 'outside and plan', and the workers of the Institute shunned it."

The Writers

The writers' community, as a whole, demonstrated a chronic indiscipline after the war which was unmatched by any other segment of Soviet society. The sources of this indiscipline were no doubt various, but there were two common factors-- the nature of literature itself, and the regime's imperfect control of it.

Writers had to deal with human beings and their relationships, in terms comprehensible to themselves and acceptable to their readers. This meant that the subject of the writer's work was man--man, not Soviet man--and human values which the shallow political philosophy he was required to serve failed to explain or even to acknowledge.

- 21 -

Secondly, the qualified editorial independence enjoyed by literary journals encouraged writers to probe for the outer limits of official tolerance. This helped to keep alive the sense of a shared problem, and contributed to a feeling of group identity among the writers.

The most dramatic episode in the postwar collision between propaganda policy on the interpretation of the war and the testimony of the writers was the article "Crocks and Potsherds," which appeared in the literary journal Oktyabr, in 1946, from the pen of its editor, F. Panferov. This article was a plaintive denunciation of the literary bureaucracy (and inescapably, though implicitly, of the political powers which supported it) for promoting a false, prettified version of the sufferings, terrors, and majestic achievements of the war.

The substance of Panferov's article was the complaint that the critics opposed any portrayal of the war which conveyed a true measure of the enormous sacrifices it had cost. In his article he described how he had questioned the generals during the last days of the war, and asked them to explain to him the nature of the victory that had been won. They could not answer, he said. Even they, the generals who had won the victory, were forced to admit that they did not fully understand the moral forces that had moved their armies. They stood before a puzzle, the sphynx of victories. Only the critics, sneered Panferov, the "crocks and potsherds," as he called them, were able to understand this great imponderable.

> For the "crocks and potsherds" all this is clear.
> "Retreat? There was no retreat. This was a planned withdrawal which exhausted the enemy."
> "But," responds the writer, "what kind of a planned withdrawal was this, when the fate of our country at one time hung by a hair. Indeed, Comrade Stalin and his fellow workers spoke to us about this."
> "Forget it! It is necessary to forget this," answer the "crocks and potsherds."
> "How forget? Perhaps it is possible to forget that the Germans were at Stalingrad, at Mozdok, at Moscow? How is it possible to forget the burdens which our people shouldered during the war? Indeed, sometimes out shoulders cracked from these burdens.

- 22 -

Panferov then recalled the terrible hardships suffered by the working people in setting up the evacuated industries in the rear. He described the hard living conditions, the rigors of winter work in the Urals, the cold which froze the palms of the workers' hands to the steel. "But here come the 'crocks and potsherds'", he wrote, "and insistently declare: 'Nonsense, nothing like this happened in our country.' The writer spreads his hands in perplexity."

Returning to the military aspect of the war, Panferov concluded his article with a discussion of the character of the enemy, and of the proper way of portraying the enemy in literature. He disputed the official tendency to deprecate the military qualities of the Germans. This, he argued, did no credit to the Soviet army, and in fact minimized the significance of the victory it had achieved. The "crocks and potsherds," he said, insist that the enemy should be portrayed as stupid, cowardly, ignorant of military matters--as a "woden head with eyes."

> But, if you will, why minimize the strength of the enemy, his resourcefulness, his rapaciousness, his cunning, his military skill, his steadiness in bat-tle, his ability to defend himself, to attack, and finally, to fight? Indeed, in depicting the enemy as a wooden head with eyes, we minimize the heroism of the Red Army. What kind of heroism is it to have beaten a wooden head with eyes? No, the enemy was strong, in his own way, able, cunning, and steady in battle. Indeed, no wooden head with eyes could have seized, if only temporarily, the whole of Eur-ope, and moved into our country hundreds of divi-sions armed from head to toe. No. And how explain the power of the enemy, his psychology--why millions went over to the fascists, if only for a time? To solve this is an extraordinarily complicated and necessary matter....

There can be no doubt that Panferov passionately be-lieved in the position he defended. Moreover, he seemd to feel that his viewpoint might prevail over the opposing view of the literary critics. He reminded his readers of the wartime words of Stalin and the party leaders; he invoked the authority of the party which "never concealed." At the time he published the article, Panferov seemed to

- 23 -

regard the interpretation of the war as not yet a completely closed issue. The objective of his article, apparently, was to bully the critics, and influence the political authorities behind them, into accepting his interpretation of the role and responsibility of literature in portraying the history of the war. No doubt, active debates on this subject had been stimulated throughout the literary community by Stalin's electoral speech earlier in the year.

The lasting signifiance of Panferov's article rests in the testament it gave of Russia's wartime experience. On the eve of the postwar campaign of falsifications and half-truths, which the regime hoped would blot out the unhappy memories of the war, one clear voice bore witness to the sufferings and sacrifices it had cost. It spoke not only for Panferov but for many of his colleagues as well, and indeed for the Russian people.

Echoes of this testimony to the truth about the war were to be heard again in the postwar period. In the last two issues of the literary journal Znamya, in 1947, there appeared a work entitled "Motherland and Foreignland: Pages from a Notebook," by A. Tvardovskiy, in which the poet attempted to recreate impressions from a lost wartime diary. It was a collection of vignettes of his wartime experiences. As the personal record of a sensitive observer, which was intended originally for his own use rather than for publication, it presented a remarkably clear view of the human features of the Soviet people in the war.

Tvardovskiy was particularly attracted by the hardiness, the sheer survival ability, of individuals in war, and he returned to this theme repeatedly. This naturally caused him to deal with characters and motivations which official propaganda pretended not to see, and laid him open to the charge that he had generalized the untypical rather than the typical features of Soviet reality. In a striking passage, he described a scene of refugee disaster during the early days:

On the first page of the notebook, I remember, I wrote down a picture which struck me at the beginning of the war, in my first encounter with those on whom a heavy burden fell in the first days. The Moscow-Kiev train stopped at a station, apparently Khutor Mikhailovskiy. Looking out the window, I saw something so strange and

- 24 -

frightening that, to this day, I cannot get rid of
the impression. I saw a field, a huge field, but
whether it was a meadow, a fallow field, a field
sown to winter or spring crops, it was impossible
to tell: the field was covered with people, lying
sitting, swarming, people with bundles, knapsacks,
suitcases, hand carts, little children. I never
saw so many suitcases, bundles, all kinds of village
household goods, hurriedly taken by people for a
journey. On this field there were perhaps five,
perhaps ten thousand people. . . . The field buzzed.
And in this drone one could hear the agitation, the
excitement caused by the recent shock, and, at the
same time, the deep, sad weariness, the numbness,
the half-sleep, that one observes in a crowded waiting room at night in a large railway junction. The
field rose, began to stir, pushed toward the right
of the way, to the train, began to rap on the win-
dows and doors of the cars, and, it seemed, had
the power to knock the cars from the rails. The
train moved. We, people in war, breaking the
strict and necessary order, pulled into the car
one woman, loaded down with bundles, holding in
her hands her two children, aged three and five
years. She was from Minsk, the wife of a commander,
and coming into the car hastened to confirm this
with documents. She was small, haggard, not at
all beautiful, except perhaps her eyes, shining
with the joy of unexpected success. She had to go
somewhere in Belaya Tserkov, to the family of her
husband. She could hardly have gotten there--
a few days later I saw that Belaya Tserkov was
abandoned by us.

Tvardovskiy's honesty extended also to self-analysis,
and produced an unusually picturesque and unflattering account of the function of the writers in the war. Feeling
the fatigue of his long tour of service, he asked himself
why his mind faltered at the task of writing once again
the story of seemingly endless battles. He compared himself and his fellow writers to a man who helped another
to chop wood by grunting for each blow of the axe. "We
grunt, and the people work. We have taken on ourselves
the function...of giving out those exclamations, 'ohs'
and 'ahs', etc., which are those of the man who fights."

For the soldier, each new battle summons up his mental and physical forces with original freshness. "But for us, grunting, all this is just more of the same thing; we have grunted for a thousand such occasions." Tvardovskiy conceded, however, that it was necessary to go on writing, because of the magnificant victories that the soldiers were winning.

The critical reaction to Tvardovskiy's notebook was swift and caustic. An article in Literary Gazette, in December, presented a biting review of the work, "The attempt to poeticize that which is foreign to the life of the people, and foreign to poetry, has led to a false and crude ideological mistake." A week later, an editorial in the same newspaper reiterated the official anger: "The whole work is impregnated with a feeling of tiredness, pacifism, a contemplative attitude toward life." In February, 1948, Literary Gazette carried a brief report of a discussion which had been held on Tvardovskiy's notebook, containing hints that opposition to the official criticism had manifested itself among the writers. The report stated that the scheduled discussion had been put off three times, and that on the fourth occasion, when the discussion was finally held, the editorial board of Znamya had absented itself from the meeting. In addition, the claim that the official evaluation of the work had been supported by the meeting was qualified: "The opinion of the majority of the speakers in large part coincided with . . . . (Italics added.) Finally, the open opposition of one speaker, a student from Moscow University, was acknowledged. Regarding the latter, the report stated:

> General agitation was called forth by the speech of a graduate student of Moscow University, V. Arkhipov. In an oily tone, he undertook to prove that there were no mistakes in "Motherland and Foreignland." Attempting by all means to protect A. Tvardovskiy from justified criticism, he ended up with openly reactionary declarations in defense of kulaks and speculators. The harmful expressions of the uninvited advocate were given a well deserved reply,...

While Tvardovskiy's work was being discussed, another wartime memoir was being published which was to set off an even more dramatic demonstration of opposition to the official line on the war. This was the diary of Olga Dzhigurda, a military doctor, which appeared in the first two

issues of Znamya in 1948, under the title "The Motor-
ship 'Kakhetia'". In the ensuing discussion of this
book, in which marked discontent with the official critical evaluation was recorded, the famous partisan leader and author of the Stalin prize winning book, Men With
a Clear Conscience, Petro Vershigora, published a strong
attack on the critics for encouraging a hypocritical
portrayal of the war. In the vigor and directness of
its attack, Vershigora's article came close to matching
the ardor of Panferov's polemic of two years before.

The diary of Dzhigurda, which precipitated the dispute, was itself a patently honest protrayal of the
thoughts, feelings, and behavior of people exposed to
war. It recorded the author's experiences as a military
doctor on a supply-hospital ship, in 1941-42, serving
the besieged city of Sevastopol and other military bases.
In simple, straightforward language, the author described
the people around her, neither embellishing their virtues
nor concealing their faults. At the very beginning, she
described the reluctance with which she and her companions
approached their assignment to the ship. "In vain,
Belokon and Vetrova entreated the duty officer to send us
to some land unit, in vain Vetrova tried to frighten
the duty officer with big names from the Air Forces, in
vain I complained of my seasickness...."

Dzhigurda's reportorial accuracy led her to record
events which were highly "untypical" by Soviet official
standards. The captain of the ship, for example, suffered a nervous breakdown and committed suicide. Two
soldiers evacuated from Sevastopol turned out to be
malingerers. "What will become of them?" asked Dzhigurda
as they were being led away. "They will be shot...(or)
...sent to a penal battalion..." she was told. Once
her roommate's sobbing woke her in the night.

"What's the matter? What's the matter with you?"
I asked anxiously.
"I cannot be alone! It's boring to be alone!" Vetrova
wailed through her tears.
I was upset
"Listen, Marya Afanas'yevna, aren't you ashamed? Just
a few days before the trip, and all you think about is
foolishness. We have to fight with pure thoughts
and a pure spirit, and all you think about is men!"
"I'm pregnant," suddenly groaned Vetrova, and fell
on the pillow and cried.

- 27 -

These "untypical" features of the book, needless to say, scandalized official opinion. Dzhigurda was accused of having failed to bring out the real spirit of the Soviet people, and of having lost her way in details. "It is not necessary to minimize the personal shortcomings of our people," said E. Knipovich, writing in Literary Gazette. "But if one is to see the main, socialist thing above all, then the petty, personal shortcomings are not blown up disproportionately...."

A discussion of the book was held early in May, 1948. The animation of the proceedings, the enthusiastic support for Dzhigurda which they demonstrated, came through even in the cryptic report of the affair which was published in Literary Gazette. A remarkable feature of the meeting was that it appeared to be organized by, and certainly provided a forum for, "people of experience," that is, those who like Dzhigurda herself had actually participated in the war. The number of military figures present, and speaking on Dzhugurda's behalf, was perhaps the most notable feature of the meeting.

In the following month, Vershigora published his formal attack on the critics. He described their reception of Dzhigurda's work as flowing from the consistently negative attitude they had always shown toward eyewitness accounts of the war. The object of his attack was to refute not simply the official evaluation of one work, but the whole system of official attitudes which had determined this evaluation. His indictment exposed the nature of the campaign the critics had waged to substitute platitudinous formulas for honest accounts of the war.

> Pseudo-classical conceptions regarding Soviet people at war, the motives for their actions and encounters, have apparently nurtured sanctimonious ideals in the critics themselves. And the critics (according to the laws of a certain reverse diffusion, perhaps) react sharply to any departure from these lacquered norms. Pharisaical critics give battle surreptiously, without undue noise, to the genre of "experience": they avoid raising the question to the level of principle, so to speak, ignore the early diaries of front-line people, or note superficially their weaknesses, and, above all, disparage their significance.

OFFICIAL USE ONLY

Vershigora cited the poverty of literature on the
siege of Leningrad as an example of the deadly influence
which had been exercised by the critics. He said that
since 1944 an honest portrayal of this great event had
been impossible. He spoke of one "highly placed conference" devoted to literature on the war, at which one
writer justifiably complained that he had not been able
to write the truth about the feat of Leningrad "since
the literary and critical channels had filled up with
people who never had a taste of blockade."

Every attempt to describe the blockade is taken by
them as slander aginst the Leningrad people.
The almost complete absence of great literature on
the worthy and necessary theme of the heroic defense of Leningrad convinces me that the aforementioned comrade is right. Crude facts (and they are
always crude, particularly for those who have not
had a whiff of them) cannot be written, and people
are apparently still ashamed to write the prettified
"little truths" which are always worse than open
lies. And the result? The needed book about the
great feat of Leningrad has not, and does not,
come!

Finally, Vershigora asserted the bold claim that
"defenders of the Fatherland" had the moral right to share
their experiences of the war with their contemporaries.
He predicted, moreover, that such first-hand accounts
would not be forgotten when the history of the war was
finally written.

Our contemporaries, who shoulder to shoulder have
forged the victory, as well as future generations
studying the past, will look into them. They will
have to look into them! Surely, the many novels,
stories and poems, and books, which are less finished
in literary style, but more convincing, not only
by virtue of the facts they contain, but also by
their faithfulness to the human feelings they portray,
will not be thrown into the backyard of history,

- 29 -

OFFICIAL USE ONLY

BODY-35

III. THE POST-STALIN REAPPRAISAL OF THE HISTORY OF THE WAR

The flurry of opposition to the official history of the war was snuffed out by 1949, and for several years thereafter a deep freeze of Stalinist orthodoxy settled over this issue. Occasional criticisms of individual authors during this period were indicative more of the insatiability of critical appetites than of any real indiscipline on the part of the individuals concerned. The increasing attention devoted to the history of the war by the press and publishing houses registered the propagandists' conviction that the subject had become stable and safe. But history in the Soviet Union was no more stable than the political forces which projected it, and with Stalin's death the image of his power reflected in history began to fade.

The Impact of Stalin's Death

The natural tendency of the Stalinist historical myths to disintegrate was accelerated by the problems which the new government faced. First, there was the succession itself: the new system of collective leadership had to be legitimized; the state administration, pulverized by Stalin, had to be reconstituted; long suppressed consumer demands had to be satisfied; a way out of the foreign policy impasse had to be found. Secondly, there were problems arising from the military-strategic situation created by the maturing of nuclear developments within the Soviet Union, and the continuing improvement of delivery capabilities in both world power blocs. Both sets of problems required a break with Stalinist tradition.

The effects of the new policy toward the first set of problems were apparent almost immediately. In propaganda, the "cult of personality" was disparaged, and the "creativity of the masses" was extolled. To be sure, the effect was less marked, and less consistent, in historical writing on the war, but there were unmistakable shifts in emphasis. Stalin's name appeared less frequently in the places where one had become accustomed to expect it, and the party was put forward as the supreme architect of victory. The role of the people in the war was also accorded a recognition which befitted their newly acknowledged status as the "creators of history."

- 30 -

More important, and longer lasting, implications for
the history of the war emerged from the second set of problems mentioned above, the reassessment of Soviet military-
strategic policies. As men who had been close to the sum-
mit of Soviet power for many years, the new leaders were
certainly not unacquainted with the strategic problems
posed by the increasing destructiveness of world armaments.
But the responsibilities of supreme authority, the removal
of Stalin's inhibiting influence, and the new evidence which
piled up during 1953, as a result of the Soviet Union's first
hydrogen bomb explosion, and also, probably, the beginning
of the study of tactics for a nuclear war in the military
maneuvers of that year, cast these problems in a new light.
In any event, clear signs of a more realistic attitude toward
the military implications of the nuclear age were manifested.
The seven year ban on the discussion of nuclear weapons was
broken, in 1954, when Red Star began a series of articles
on the tactical uses of the new weapons, and defense against
them. During the same period, a broad discussion of military
science, reflecting strong tendencies toward a rejuvenation
of military thought, was carried on in the General Staff
journal, Military Thought.

On the political level, the impact of the new strategic
situation was reflected in Malenkov's efforts to damp down
the sparks which might set off an international conflagra-
tion--which, in his words of 1954, would mean the "destruction of world civilization." The circumstances surrounding
this declaration strongly suggest that Malenkov meant it as
a powerful argument in defense of his policies. It was made
just four days after the first open opposition to his regime
had been signalized in the Soviet press.* It was a carefully
calculated statement, since it revised a long held, and often
repeated Soviet doctrine, which Malenkov himself had helped
to formulate, that a new war would mean the destruction of
world capitalism alone. The indications are strong that it
expressed not only his own belief in the unacceptibility of
nuclear war, but his hope that others within the Soviet

---

* Trud, March 8, 1954. A commerative article on Stalin
contained the first of the revised "war records," of which there
would be various others in the next two years, listing only Khrushchev and Bulganin, of the then collective leaders, as among
the party leaders sent to the front during the war.

- 31 -

Union, the lesser party leaders and intellectuals, would be persuaded to accept his view.

Malenkov's specific prescription for Soviet policy in the nuclear age was repudiated when he resigned in February 1955, but the military-strategic considerations which had given rise to it continued to preoccupy his successors. Moreover, the power struggle by which the Bulganin-Khrushchev succession was engineered, by placing the military in a temporarily more independent position, had the effect of stimulating the tendencies toward a fresh look at military realities which the Malenkov regime had initiated. The return of experienced military officers to high administrative posts in the defense establishment, which had been going on since the last year of Stalin's life, and particularly the appointment of Marshal Zhukov as Minister of Defense in February 1955, further accelerated these tendencies. During the next few months, the enhanced professionalism and realism which these developments brought to the sphere of military thought, resulted in important revisions in military doctrine and military history.

The harbinger of the new era in military thought was an article by Marshal of Tank Troops Rotmistrov, which appeared in the February issue of Military Thought, revising the reigning Soviet doctrine on the significance of the suprise factor in war. Ever since the early days of the war, when Stalin propounded his doctrine of the permanently operating factors which determine the outcome of war, the significance of the surprise factor had been deprecated in Soviet military theory. In wartime propaganda and subsequently, the early successes of of Germans were ascribed to the "temporary" factor of surprise, which had no significance for the final outcome of the war, once the permanently operating factors (the stability of the rear, the morale of the army, the quantity and quality of divisions, the armament of the army, the organizational abilities of the commanding staff) came into play. In Rotmistrov's article, for the first time, the relationship between the permanently operating fuctors and the temporary factors (of which surprise was the principal one) was clearly shifted to heighten the significance of the latter. For the first time, the factor of suprise was accorded a significance which an age of nuclear weapons and transcontinental bombers made prudent and necessary. The reasons for this shift of doctrine were explained some years later by a military author writing in Red Star. "The appearance of nuclear weapons,"

- 32 -

he said, "and the possibility for their mass employment against troops and targets in the rear, produced different opinions on the significance of the surprise attack in a future war, and on measures for opposing such an attack. This prompted some military writers to engage in an investigation of the significance of the factor of surprise in modern war." Marshal Rotmistrov, it seems, was the first to have the courage to voice the opinions which these considerations produced in him. Subsequent developments showed that he was not alone in his views.

The Revisionary Movement of 1955

The revision of the history of the war which unfolded in 1955 was a direct result of the military-strategic revaluations which we have been examining. It reflected the Soviet leaders' apprehension that the Soviet people, and the Soviet military establishment, were being poorly prepared for the kind of war which they now foresaw as a possibility by the unrealistic portrayal of the last year. This propaganda, they felt, encouraged the dangerous illusion that war was easy, and conditioned military officers to feel that retreats, and slow attritional methods, were normal means of conducting war. In a word, the official history of the war compounded the errors which Soviet military doctrine had committed. As Military Thought put it at this time, and as it would be reiterated in other writings during the year, the official history had led "not only to distorting the actual military events of 1941, but to the idealization of this form of combat, and incorrectly orients our military cadres to the possibilities of repeating it in a future war."

The first full statement of the new version of the war which these considerations produced appeared in a lead editorial of Military Thought, in March, 1955. The main thesis presented was that fresh and original thought was needed to keep the Soviet military establishment responsive to the demands of contemporary military realities. It condemned the slavish attitude toward Stalin, which, it said, obtained among military writers. It asked scornfully why Stalin's thesis on the permanently operating factors should have been considered a new contribution to military science. "Why was this permitted?"

it asked. "For no other reason than that our military-scientific workers, academicians, military editors, our military press, are afraid to call things by their right names, and say anything new." The editors of Military Thought themselves, the editorial admitted, shared this guilt. They had held back the publication of Rotmistrov's article on surprise because of their fear of posing new questions.

The main content of the new version of the war which this article defined, and later articles elaborated, was that the early period of the war was a defeat for the Soviet army, rather than a prelude to victory. Criticism focussed on the doctrine of "active defense," on the old official claim that the operations of the first period of the war had been conceived ahead of time, and skillfully applied to bring about the defeat of the enemy. In fact, there never was such a plan, it was now admitted. "What the case was in fact we all well remember. Our experiences in that period, so desperate for our country, are sufficiently fresh in our memories." The doctrine of active defense, it was stated, concealed the mistakes which had been committed during that period, and the defeats that had been suffered. It also denied due credit to the soldiers and people for their patriotism, courage, and staunchness, and to the command-personnel for their skill. "It is necessary to put an end to this mistaken concept of the initial period of the war as quickly as possible, since in fact the operations of that period, in the main, had the character of withdrawal operations."

The impetus to revision which this article set in motion carried somewhat beyond the program it defined. Two months later, the second period of the war was being subjected to critical review as well. Colonel General F. Kurochkin, writing in the May issue of Military Thought, found glossing and over-simplification in the way the "ten Stalinist crushing blows" had been presented in official historical literature. Only a few of these operations, he said, were carried out according to plan. Some took longer than expected, others developed into operations larger than had been foreseen. Kurochkin presented the Stalingrad battle in an unusual way, also, in that he gave no indication that German strategy had aimed at the envelopment of Moscow.

- 34 -

The role of Stalin in the war was naturally affected by
this revisionary movement, although the depreciation of his
services did not proceed as far as certain statements in the
original Military Thought editorial had seemed to imply.
He continued to be accorded honor as the head of the country
and the leader of the Armed Forces, although the adulatory
phrases which had surrounded his name in past propaganda were
toned down or removed. Kurochkin provided a precise formula
showing how the new history allocated the credits for victory
among the major political elements of Soviet society:

> The Communist Party of the Soviet Union was
> the leading and directing force in the heroic strug-
> gle of the Soviet people against the German fascist
> aggressors, and raised outstanding commanders, who,
> headed by J. V. Stalin, demonstrated strategic and
> operational leadership....The fundamental creator of
> the victory over fascist Germany...was the Soviet
> people....

Finally, the role of the Allies in the war was broached
indirectly in the new history. This reflected, however, no
concern for fairness or honesty, but the practical desirabil-
ity of knowing the strengths and weaknesses of a possible
future enemy. The original Military Thought editorial condemned the ideological inhibitions which had conditioned So-
vied military writers to look upon non-Marxist literature as
beneath their attention. "It is necessary decisively to con-
demn such a view. This is nothing but pride and arrogance."
Behind the editorial's concern in this matter, it was clear,
were the same pratical considerations which had prompted its
attack on the official interpretation of the war. "It should
be sufficiently clear to everyone that it is impossible to
develop national military science without knowing well the
military-theoretical views of the adversary."

While these developments were taking place in the closed
circle of military specialists, a somewhat blurred image of
the new history was being presented to the Soviet people. The
public presentation of the revised history was complicated
by the recent political upheaval. The stimulus to factional-
ism within the upper reaches of the Soviet hierarchy which
had accompanied the change of government, and the temporary
slackening of political control which had followed it, posed
an invitation to politically-inclined military leaders to

maneuver for position in the new regime. The historical interpretation of the war provided one platform on which this maneuvering could take place, since allegiance to one or another political leader could be indicated by the way in which the war was treated. The fact that the Khrushchev faction, for tactical reasons in its struggle with Malenkov, had associated its program with Stalinist symbols left an opening for those who wished to declare their loyalty to Khrushchev to do so by resisting any revision of the war which had anti-Stalinist implications. This was presumably the reason why some military leaders, particularly Marshal Konev, in his speech at the Bolshoi theater on the Tenth Anniversary of victory, made little or no concession the the new interpretation of the war. On the whole, however, the majority of articles which appeared at this time showed some impress of the revisionary movement.

A clearer indication of the import of the new movement was given to the two groups which, apart from the military, were most affected by the history of the war, the writers and the historians. At the end of May, 1955, a meeting of writers was held to explain the contemporary role of the military, and the responsibilities of literature in presenting that role and in cultivating the soldierly and civic virtues which supported it. An essential element of this explanation was the presentation of the revised view of the war which these practical considerations had produced among the military theorists themselves. The meeting was sponsored by the Union of Writers, but it was obviously initiated by the Main Political Administration of the Ministry of Defense. The keynote was sounded by the deputy chief of the Main Political Administration, Lieutenant General Shatilov, in an article which appeared in Literary Gazette on the eve of the meeting.

Shatilov placed great emphasis throughout on the danger of attack by the West, and the greatly increased peril which this posed for the Soviet Union in view of the new conditions of warfare created by nuclear weapons and improved delivery systems. This, he said, gave new significance to the question of surprise in war, and required a more careful consideration

- 36 -

of the role which surprise had played in the past. In particular, he said, it was necessary to show how the factor of surprise had dominated the first period of the last war, since a false portrayal of this period might encourage false notions about the nature of a future war.

> In connection with this, it is necessary to point out that in our literature devoted to the Great Patriotic War, the first period of military operations is often idealized, portrayed as a period of operations conceived in classic forms as a so-called "active defense," and authors, contradicting real facts, attempt to depict the matter as though this "active defense" had been planned ahead of time and had entered into the calculations of our command.... A primitive interpretation of the initial period of the war, which distorts living reality, wherever it takes place -- in scientific works or in artistic works -- cannot be tolerated, since it distorts historical truth, and incorrectly orients our people, creating the impression that such precedents might, and even should, be repeated in the future.

The published reports of the main speakers, and the reports of the sessions, presented reiterations of this theme, and also a hint or two of reactions stimulated in the writer's community by the new atmosphere. In the main the sessions bore an official stamp (an impression enhanced by the absence of the principal wartime writers, such as Simonov, Grossman, Leonov), and the meeting was chiefly significant as a sounding-board for the new official line.

The historians received their briefing on the new interpretation of the war in the lead editorial of Questions of History in June. This was the first formal public directive for a thorough review of the history of the war, and in some respects it went beyond the program of revision outlined in the military press. Besides repeating the by now standard call for a revision of the first period of the war, it also demanded a more balanced appraisal of the Moscow and Stalingrad battles (since describing them as turning-points of the war tended to diminish the significance of the Kursk and subsequent battles), and urged a fuller account of the role of the Allies. The latter point was qualified, however, by the linked

- 37 -

argument that this would help dispel the "reactionary falsifications of history" promoted by the imperialist press. Finally, it spelled out the reasons for this call for revision.

> Study and popularization of the history of the
> Great Patriotic War will help strengthen the Soviet
> people's military preparedness to crush any imperialist
> aggressor, and will help further to train the Soviet
> people in unshakable faith in the victory of their just
> cause, and in ardent Soviet patriotism and proletarian
> internationalism.

This article was the principal manifesto of the revisionary movement in 1955. During the remainder of the year there
were few signs that the revision was being pursued vigorously,
although another article by Rotmistrov, in November, showed
that the theoretical considerations affecting the factor of
surprise, which had provoked the historical revision in the
first place, continued to prevail in military circles. The
Essays on the History of the Great Patriotic War, the first
full-length history of the war by professional historians to
be published in the Soviet Union, which came out later in
the year, showed very little effects of the 1955 revisionary
movement. This, together with the general disappearance of
the issue from the Soviet press, suggests that cautionary
political influences, as well as irresolution within the collective leadership as to Stalin's role in history, had resulted
in slowing down the tinkering with the history of the war. This
was, however, only a temporary pause, as events of the following
year were to show. As the Twentieth Party Congress approached,
new tendencies toward a break with the past appeared which resulted in giving fresh impetus to a reconsideration of the
history of the war.

The Revisionary Movement of 1956

The revisionary movement of 1956 followed the channels
that had been cut by the military historians of 1955, but it
was sponsored and sustained by new forces, and it served goals
that were broader than the military-strategic considerations
that had defined the earlier initiative. Moreover, it generated
a momentum that carried it beyond the limits envisioned by
the official revision of 1955, and indeed beyond the designs
of the official sponsors of 1956.

The central thrust of the new movement was the general
break with Stalin which was dramatized by the Twentieth Party
Congress. As we have seen, a gradual withdrawal from Stalinist
traditions and Stalinist methods of leadership had been taking
place since 1953, and although cautious downgradings of Stalin's
historical role had accompanied this process, no clear and
definitive disavowal of Stalin had been attempted.

Strong tendencies toward the revaluation of the Stalinist
historical legacy appeared even before the Twentieth Party Congress opened, and assumed a programmatic character at the conference of the readers of Questions of History, which was held
at the end of January, 1956. Accurately anticipating the mood
of the Congress which was to convene two weeks later, the conference outlined a revisionary program touching a broad range
of established Soviet historical attitudes. Stalin's name
appears not to have been mentioned in the leading speeches;
Lenin was repeatedly extolled as the source of Soviet historical traditions; implicit criticism of Stalin's textbook on
the history of the party (the "Short Course") was advanced;
the cult of personality in history was condemned. Even sacre-
sanct Soviet historical attitudes -- toward the bourgeoisie,
and toward the intra-party struggles of the pre-revolutionary
and revolutionary periods -- were affected by the revisionary
impulse. The reports of the conference made clear that a
core of liberalizing historians, led by E. N. Burdzhalov,
the deputy editor of Questions of History, was preparing to
dismantle a large part of the historical scaffolding which
had been erected around Stalin's image.

The history of the war was one part of the historical
legacy that was brought up for review, although it was not
a major preoccupation of the conference. Burdzhalov touched
the subject briefly in his broad ranging critique of past
historical attitudes, and complained that "the difficulties
of the first period" had not been revealed in standing works
on the war. More relevant to the main thrust of his argument,
and also carrying implications for the history of the war,
was his call for a fresh approach to the study of the West.
"The USA has progressive traditions, as well as reactionary,"
he noted. Others indicated their favorable attitude toward
a new history of the war by praising the revisionary editorial
which had appeared in Questions of History in 1955. Still
others complained of the situation that had prevailed in the

past: the closing down of the military historical section of the History Institute, the inaccessability of archive documents, the "schematization, vulgarization, departure from historical truth, the idealization of past military figures, the personality cult," which had characterized military history.

The Twentieth Party Congress encouraged this movement not only by giving it official auspices, but by supplying the substantive criticism of Stalin which served as the solvent of traditional historical attitudes. Khrushchev's secret speech, which portrayed Stalin as ignorant of military matters, and as criminally responsible for the initial unpreparedness of the Soviet Union and for subsequent defeats, was quickly made known to party members, and, indirectly, to the politically literate elements of the Soviet population. Beginning a few weeks after the adjournment of the Congress and continuing for several months thereafter, the Soviet press gave numerous signs of the shock impact which these revelations had had throughout the Soviet Union. Reports of lower party meetings, which began to appear on 19 March, and a rash of editorials which blossomed on the themes of "party unity" and "Leninist principles," were liberally sprinkled with angry charges against "rotten elements," "demagogues," "leftists," etc., who were allegedly using the revelations as pretexts for attacks against the party.

One charge deserves special mention here because of its relevance to the historiography of the war. This was the charge that party members had used the denigration of Stalin as a vehicle for the disparagement of authority in general, and in particular in its Soviet form of one-man command. Repeatedly, from early April until as late as August, the party press fulminated against those who denied "all authority," who sought to undermine "party discipline," who expressed a "petty-bourgeois denial of the role of leaders in state, party, and economic work," who denied the "principle of one-man leadership," who attempted "to minimize the role of authority."

A dramatic incident affecting the history of the war took place at this time. This was the open dispute between two major military organs regarding the way in which the new data affecting Stalin's role in history, and the general revisionary spirit being sponsored by the party, should be applied to the interpretation of the war. In April, Military Herald published an editorial which presented a far-reaching revision of the history of the war, bolder than anything that had been seen in

- 40 -

public before. Its main point was that the early defeats of
the Soviet army were due not to the surprise of the German
attack, but to the negligence of the Soviet government in
failing to take the precautionary measures which elementary
prudence, and ample intelligence warnings, indicated were
necessary. Included in this indictment was the charge, first
made by Khrushchev in his secret speech, that the prewar industrial planning of the Soviet Union had not been properly
geared to defense needs. Secondary points of the article
ran a broad gamut of criticism tending to deprecate, or even
to debunk, the past official historiography of the war. Among
these points was an unprecedented criticism of the concept
of the counteroffensive, as it had been applied to the interpretation of the Stalingrad battle. From the accounts of this
battle sponsored by official propaganda, Military Herald scornfully observed, the conclusion seemed justified that "it was
fitting and even proper that Soviet troops should have re-
treated to Stalingrad, since this caused the enemy to 'expose'
his flanks." Finally, in an egregious understatement, which
must have touched exposed political nerves, the editorial
noted that there had been "a lack of proper attention to so
important a question as the casualties and losses of material
in various battles and operations...."

Shortly thereafter, on the anniversary of Victory Day,
Red Star, the official organ of the Ministry of Defense, came
out with a sharp rebuttal of these charges, and a direct criticism of Military Herald. It was "surprised and grieved," it
said, by the incorrect and harmful opinions contained in the
Military Herald editorial. It described as "strange and un-
convincing" the assertions of Military Herald that the defeats of the early period of the war were caused by the unpreparedness of the Soviet armed forces. Moreover, it said,
the question of the industrial preparedness of the country,
as presented in Military Herald, was "grossly" distorted. The
reasons for Red Star's reaction were not hard to find. In the
first place, it reflected the wounded vanity of the military
chiefs, who had shared some responsibility for the state of
the nation's defenses on the eve of the war and who were now
for the first time beginning to feel the bite of the critical
spirit they had helped to loose. Secondly, it reflected a
concern, quite natural to the conservative military establishment in the stormy atmosphere of the post-Twentieth Party
Congress period, that the denigration of Stalin was being
carried to the point where the moral basis of authority in
the armed forces was being shaken. Red Star made this concern explicitly clear.

- 41 -

While this drama was being played, Questions of History
was imparting its own vigorous thrust to the revisionary movement. In its April issue, it published a directive article
calling for a broad review of virtually the whole historical
legacy of the Stalin era, including the history of the war.
In May, it published a more detailed attack on the past official history of the war, in the form of a critique, by Colonel E. A. Boltin, of the Essays on the History of the Great
Patriotic War. This article supported and elaborated the
main tenets of the Military Herald editorial, and also introduced an entirely new element into the revisionary move-
ment--a call for a more appreciative evaluation of the contributions of the Allies in the war. The scope of revision
proposed in this matter was conveyed by specific criticisms
which the author made of the Essays. The Essays had failed
to show: the relationship between the Great Patriotic War and
the Second World War; the "liberational, antifascist character" of the Second World War even before the USSR entered
it; the contribution made by the anti-Hitler coalition to the
USSR; the "positive results" of the North African operations;
all the "military and political importance" of the Allied invasion of Europe; the actions of "our partners in the anti-
Hitler coalition" in the Pacific War. The author could well
say, in line with the spirit expressed in these criticisms,
that there was "the greatest historic importance in the fact
that the Soviet socialist state. . .gained allies among the
majority of these /capitalist7 states in the war against world
fascism."

In the meantime, the issue raised by Red Star, which had
remained unresolved for two months, was finally settled. In
July, after the publication of the central committee document on overcoming the cult of personality, which indicated
that the party intended to push on with the anti-Stalin campaign, the party's theoretical organ, Kommunist, intervened
to rebuke Red Star for its sally against Military Herald.
Kommunist went down the line in supporting the main theses
of the Military Herald editorial, including the delicate issue of the prewar industrial preparedness of the country.
The shortages of equipment which developed in the early period of the war were the result, it admitted, of "a serious
omission in the planned development of military industry in
the prewar years." It also endorsed, incidentally, in somewhat less enthusiastic language, the more generous appraisal
of the role of the Allies in the war given by Questions of
History.

- 42 -

This was the highpoint of the 1956 revisionary movement. In the following months it rapidly lost momentum. The nucleus of conservative opposition in the historical community, which had put up a stubborn resistance to the revisionary movement from the beginning, began to gain the upper hand in the fall. While the issues in this running battle concerned mainly internal party history, the gradual ascendancy of the conservative point of view on these issues had the effect of placing the whole revisionist movement on the defensive. More important for the fortunes of the revisionist movement were the changes in the political climate which took place in the latter half of 1956. The adverse political repercussions of the anti-Stalin campaign throughout the world undoubtedly exerted a depressing influence on the anti-Stalinist ardor of the Soviet leadership. After the Hungarian revolt, the anti-Stalin campaign, with its attendant revisionary impulses, was sharply curbed. Thereafter, little more was heard about the revision of the history of the war in the Soviet Union, until the subject was reopened, under more controlled conditions, toward the end of 1957.

IV.   THE CONSOLIDATION OF THE POST-STALIN REVISIONS

The need for a readjustment of the energizing impulses of the Twentieth Party Congress to the more permanent goals and requirements of the Soviet system of power was evident to the Soviet leadership after 1956. In the field of military thought, the regime did not wish to renounce the progress made in the revisionary movements of 1955 and 1956, but it could not tolerate the political brushfires which had accompanied, and had in part been fed by, this process.

The Shifting Propaganda Line

In 1957, Soviet writing on World War II showed clear signs of the uncertainty and tendency toward retrenchment which affected Soviet policy generally after the events of the fall of 1956. The Armed Forces Day articles in February, for example, appeared to be cut from different patterns, and registered a number of partial retreats from the advanced revisionary positions of 1956.

Marshal Malinovskiy, in the major article of the day, while acknowledging the massive defeats of the Soviet Army during the early days, took pains to exonerate the Soviet military command from responsibility for these failures. Turning the Military Herald statement of 1956 (that the war "could have come as no surprise" to the Soviet leadership) into a defense of the military leadership rather than an accusation, he wrote: "It must be said directly that this (the German attack) was not a surprise to the Supreme Soviet Military Command; many measures aimed at heightening the military preparedness and fighting capacity of the Soviet Armed Forces, at reorganizing them, were in the stage of being carried out and conducted at the time when fascist Germany attacked...," Marshal Meretskov departed even further from the spirit of 1956, sloughing over the early defeats, and focussing attention on traditional inspiritional themes. He even suggested a partial rehabilitation of Stalin. "This historic victory was achieved under the leadership of the Communist Party and its Central Committee, led by J. V. Stalin." Marshal Moskalenko, writing in Red Star, barely mentioned the Second World War, and said nothing of the early defeats.

In general, there was very little press attention to
the history of the war in 1957, perhaps less than during any
comparable period since the end of the war. Ceremonial occasions which in the past had usually drawn attention to this
subject were passed by in 1957 with few reminiscences of this
kind. Even the Victory Day observances were muted, and Zhukov's Order of the Day on that occasion, and the accompanying
editorials, drew attention to the future rather than to the
past. The little that was written, moreover, was strongly defensive in tone. The Victory Day issue of Red Star was fairly
typical of the Soviet press during the year in this respect.
The only article on the war which it presented was a critique
of Western "falsifications" of history, and the only allusion
to the failures of the first period it contained was the equi-
vocal statement that "the socialist regime permitted our people...to overcome successfully the shortcomings in preparations for repelling the attack of the aggressors..."

While the passage of time had undoubtedly reduced the political importance of the war for Soviet propaganda, the character of press commentary on this subject is difficult to explain except as the result of leadership uncertainty as to the
proper line to pursue. The whole matter of the interpretation
of the war was, as we have seen, closely connected with the
question of Stalin's role in history, and the sober second
thoughts which had arisen on this subject could not but affect
the willingness of the leadership to continue with the revisionary initiatives of 1956. In addition to the disturbing
impact which the denigration of Stalin had had within the Soviet Union, it had given ammunition to those in the satellites
who questioned the necessity and competence of the Soviet
Union's leadership of the world Communist movement. To the
Soviet leaders, in this circumstance, it mush have seemed difficult enough to preserve their own reputations unsullied without drawing attention to a dramatic example of Soviet leadership incompetence in the past. By the end of 1957, however,
the outlines of a firmer position on the history of the war began to appear. Beginning at this time, the volume of press
material on the history of the war began to increase, and it
showed consistent and well-defined tendencies.

The most prominent feature of the new material was the
blend of candor and caution it displayed in dealing with the
initial period of the war. Acknowledgements of the failures
of the first period were again made, but they were closely
linked with arguments calculated to draw attention to the achievements

- 45 -

of the party and people in overcoming them. The quick shifting of focus from defeats to victories in these references
became almost formularized. Marshal Grechko, writing in Red
Star on Victory Day, 1958, expressed it in the following way:
"A particularly bitter experience fell to the lot of the Soviet people in the initial period of the war, when the Soviet
Armed Forces were forced to conduct difficult defensive battles. However these failures did not break the militant
spirit of the Soviet Army and Navy, did not shake the staunchness of our people and their unlimited faith in the victory
of our just cause." Marshal Malinovsky spoke more fully of
the first period in his Armed Forces Day speech, of the same
year, but he also emphasized the positive aspect of the country's quick recovery from these failures. "The attack of the
German fascists on the Soviet Union was effected at a time
when our Armed Forces were still in the process of reorganization and technical rearmament.... Courageously battling with
the overwhelming forces of the adversary in the extremely unfavorable circumstances which arose in the initial period of
war due to a whole number of causes and mistakes, they suffered
heavy losses in personnel and fighting equipment, and were
forced reluctantly to retreat into the interior of the country.
In the face of the mortal danger hanging over our country, the
Communist party aroused the whole Soviet people to a just defensive war against the fascist aggressors."

While technically faithful to the contents of the 1956 revisionary historiography, these references, it will be seen,
were defensive in tone, and more concerned with making clear
the Soviet Union's wartime achievements than with criticizing
past historical exaggerations of it. This same purpose was
manifest in the many articles which appeared after 1957 criticizing alleged bourgeois falsifications of history. The main
complaint in all of these articles was that the exaggeration
of secondary battles and theaters in which Allied forces had
participated resulted in the minimization of the Soviet Union's
role in the war. This complaint was often linked with a more
aggressive disparagement of the Allied contribution to the victory. An article of this kind, in Vestnik Vozdushnogo Flota,
No. 6, 1959, for example, disputed the value of the Allied supply of aircraft to the USSR during the war. It emphasized the
poor quality of "Hurricanes" and "Tomahawks", claimed that "Air-
ocobras" were the most accident-prone of all wartime fighters,
and implied that planes coming to Russia were intentionally
damaged in transit.

- 46 -

This flood of criticisms of "bourgeois falsifications of history" also illustrated another aspect of the Soviet attitude toward the history of the war. Most, if not all, of these criticisms were directed at works which had been translated and published in the Soviet Union, and the criticisms thus were tacitly directed at the liberal publication policy which had permitted those books to appear. A naval captain, writing in Izvestia on 25 June 1958, for example, deplored the "incomprehensibly indulgent and careless attitude of our publishing houses to such specimens of falsification of history." Of the two publishing houses principally engaged in this activity, the Military Publishing House and the Publishing House of Foreign Literature, the latter came in for the sharpest barbs in this respect. It must be stressed, however, that no direct criticism of the policy of publishing translations of foreign literature was expressed, but only of the failure of editors and publishing houses to supply adequate critical forewords and footnotes.

The above examples bring out clearly enough the main tendencies of the new Soviet line. It was characterized chiefly by a conservative concern to bolster the party's historical reputation, and to preserve intact the traditional image of Soviet wartime achievements. At the same time, it sought to retain the gains in historical objectivity achieved in 1955 and 1956. In other words, it encouraged a technically accurate account of the military history of the war, in a framework of political interpretations which removed the unfavorable reflections on the party itself.

Publishing Activity on the War

There is similar evidence of the development of Soviet attitudes in book publishing activity, which in 1957 began to assume a bulk and character which gave it independent significance as an expression of official policy.

Important changes in publishing activity relating to the war were set in motion by the 1955 and 1956 revisionary movements. One factor in these changes may have been a more liberal military classification policy which permitted material to appear which formerly would have been limited to restricted publications. In any event, detailed studies of wartime military experiences, of the kind which once might have borne the legend

"For Generals, Admirals, and officers of the Soviet Armed Forces only," began to come out in significant numbers after 1956. Most of these books were published by the Ministry of Defense, and some of them were sponsored by the Frunze and Voroshilov academies. They included analyses of small unit actions in different types of operations, studies of specific tactical problems, and unit and campaign histories.

The professional purposes underlying the publication of this literature were expressed in the foreward to a typical example brought out in 1958. Major General V. D. Vasilevskiy, the editor of a book entitled Battle Operations of an Infantry Regiment, explained the aims of the publication in the following way:

> It is impermissible to underrate the rich experience gained in the waging of battles, much less to forget it. Despite the fact that a new weapon has appeared at the present time which, along with other factors, has had a great influence on our views regarding the conduct of battle operations in contemporary conditions, the experience of the Great Patriotic War has not lost its significance. The Great Patriotic War provided much that is instructive which sould be learned and reflected in organization and training, and in the conduct of contemporary battles.

The content of the book was also typical of the bulk of this literature. It presented a collection of studies of individual infantry actions, providing exact data on the numbers of men and weapons involved. Each study was concluded by a brief critique identifying the shortcomings and failures displayed in the conduct of the action. The critiques were usually specific and technical, but included occasional observations which perhaps had more general significance. These studies provided no information on the numbers of Soviet casualties suffered, which suggested that this sensitive subject was still under strict political censorship.

Another category of literature which began to appear in increasing quantities as a result of the revisionary movements of 1955 and 1956 was the translations of foreign works on the war. The authors chosen for translation included German generals who had fought against the Soviet Union, Western military experts who dealt in an interpretive way with the Second World

- 48 -

War as a whole, and Western specialists who dealt with particular aspects of the war remote from Soviet experience. Important documentary collections, such as the wartime correspondence of Roosevelt, Churchill, and Stalin, and the records-of the Nuremburg trials, also came out at this time.

As we have noted above, some criticism of this liberal publication policy began to be expressed in 1958 in connection with the general conservative tendency of Soviet political attitudes at that time. However, these criticisms, which were directed at the manner in which this material was presented, were accompanied by explicit approvals of the general policy of translating and publishing foreign works on the war.

General histories of the war did not immediately emerge in any quantities from the revisionary movements of 1955 and 1956, although some initial steps in this direction were taken. Both the Frunze and Voroshilov military academies brought out individual collections of materials at this time which were designed as a basis for such a history. These publications, which were restricted in circulation (and bore approximately the same title--A Collection of Materials on the History of Soviet Military Art in the Great Patriotic War) presented selections of previously published articles from such sources as Military Thought, and the Large Soviet Encyclopedia, conveniently arranged to provide the best available information on various phases and topics of the war. A more ambitious work, by a collective of authors headed by P. A. Zhilin, was brought out by the Ministry of Defense under the title The Most Important Operations of the Great Patriotic War. This book, which was given to the printer in July 1955, and signed for the press in January 1956, reflected and documented the candid appraisal of the first period of the war which became orthodox in 1955. Thereafter, the cautionary influences, which we have noted above in other connections, apparently intervened to hold up any similar historical documentation of the broader revisionary movement of 1956.

The key event in stimulating a further development of the historiography of the war was a decision of the Central Committee in the fall of 1957 authorizing the Marxism-Leninism Institute to prepare a five-volume history of the war. P. N. Pospelov, a candidate member of the party presidium, with general responsibilities in ideological and propaganda matters, was named as the supervisor of the project. A new sector of the history of the Great Patriotic War was set up in the Marxism-Leninism Institute with a group of authors headed by Major General E. A. Boltin. Periodic reports on

- 49 -

the progress of the work indicates that the scope of the history
has been expanded to include a sixth volume, mainly devoted to a
critique of Western historiography of the war. The work is
scheduled to be completed during the period 1960-1962.

The Central Committee decree of autumn 1957, in addition
to authorizing a textbook had the effect of focussing the attention and efforts of the whole military-historical community
on the subject of the history of the war, and of starting something like a race to exploit the newly opened market. The first
results of the competition have been registered. Two of the new
books, G. A. Deborin's, The Second World War, and B. S. Tel'puk-
hovskiy's The Great Patriotic War of the Soviet Union, 1941-1945,
deal largely with the political aspects of the war, and register
the generally conservative trends which have become evident in
this area since 1957. A third book, S. P. Platonov's The Second
World War, deals more directly with the military aspects of the
war, and reflects the relative objectivity which continues to
prevail in this aspect of the historiography of the war.

The Most Recent Historiography

Platonov's The Second World War, published in 1958, is a
large book, covering almost 1,000 pages of text, and including
a separate volume of unusually well-printed maps, cross-refer-
enced to the relevant sections of the narrative. It covers not
only the events on the eastern front, but includes sections on
the battle of the Atlantic, the North African operations, the
Normandy invasion, etc. Parts of the narrative dealing with
the Soviet-German war are based on documents and materials of
the History Administration of the General Staff, which, for
the first time in Soviet published literature, are specifically
identified in the bibliography of this volume. The author's
foreword tells us that the book is intended for generals, admirals, and officers of the Soviet armed forces.

Platonov's account of the initial period of the war adheres
closely to the general line which emerged from the revisonary
movements of 1955 and 1956. It includes the admission that Soviet industry on the eve of the war was improperly geared to
defense needs, that the Soviet army was unprepared for the German attack, and that the retreats of the first period were forced
upon the Soviet army by its unpreparedness and inadequacy.

- 50 -

The delicate question of the industrial preparedness of the country on the eve of the war is treated approximately as it was in 1956. It is claimed that the status of industry, as a whole, was good, but that the production of military equipment was obstructed by planning mistakes. According to Platnov: "The transition of industry to a broad production of new military equipment and armaments was carried out with great delay, and the tempo of its reconstruction was slow and inconsistent with the growing danger of an armed attack by Hitlerite Germany on the USSR." (p. 163).

The military unpreparedness of the country is described with equal candor. It is stated that the Soviet border units were undermanned, that they were largely composed of new recruits, and that they were not deployed in assigned defensive lines. They were also psychologically unprepared for war, it is said, due to the failure of the government to warn the staffs of the border districts that a danger of war existed. Finally, it is admitted that the armament of the Soviet troops, though superior to the Germans in quantity, was far inferior in quality. The wealth of detail which Platonov provides on this question presents a picture of stupidity and complacency on the Soviet side which is more damning than anything previously published in the Soviet Union and perhaps even outside the USSR.

Platonov spares little in his account of the early defeats. He gives exact figures on the extent and tempo of the German advance which bring out in a graphic way the scale of the initial catastrophe. He also portrays the ineffectiveness of the Soviet military resistance. "Thus," he says, "neither in the border area, nor on the line of the western Dvina, nor at the Pskov and Ostrovskiy fortified regions, could the troops of the Northwestern Front hold back the adversary."

The freshness of Platonov's account is revealed particularly by his treatment of issues on which no public leadership statement exists. The battle of Smolensk provides a case in point. Soviet historians had always sought to portray the long German delay at Smolensk as the result of stubborn Soviet resistance when, in fact, it stemmed also from a German decision to shift the directions of its advance to other sectors of the front. Platonov mentions Soviet resistance as a factor in stopping the Germans, but he makes it clear that the pause on the central front in July and August was the result of a voluntary German decision, and he cites the German military orders bearing upon this decision.

The relative objectivity of Platonov's account, illustrated by these examples, affected not only his description of the external course of events, but also his analysis of the factors which influenced these developments. Past Soviet accounts, for example, had always laid great stress on the alleged numerical superiority of the Germans during the early part of the war as a reason for Soviet failures. Platonov goes a long way toward correcting this distortion. While he disputes German claims of a dramatic shift in the manpower ratio during the first campaign (Tippelskirch claimed that the Russians enjoyed a twenty-fold superiority at Moscow) he does admit that a slight shift to the advantage of the Soviet side had taken place, at the jumping-off points of the Moscow counteroffensive, by the end of November. He also assigns due weight to the variety of accidental factors which told in the final German failure to take Moscow. Unlike previous accounts which had reserved all credit in this event for Soviet staunchness and military skill, he speaks freely of German mistakes and difficulties. He points out, for example, that the quality of the German army had deteriorated badly by the time of the Moscow battle, with its infantry divisions reduced to half strength and its tank forces badly depleted. Moreover, in a startling admission for a Soviet author, he states correctly that the Germans "did not have winter uniforms, and that the equipment and a part of the infantry and artillery weapons were not adapted for use in winter conditions." (p. 248)

This history is, of course, far from a truly objective account by Western standards. In general, it is least satisfactory where the narrative of military events becomes entangled with the political line on the West. This is illustrated by Platonov's treatment of the forewarning of the Soviet government of the German invasion plans. He speaks of the "miscalculations of J. V. Stalin in the evaluation of the situation," and complains that the "catastrophe" of the first days "could have been avoided if the troops of the border districts had been forewarned in good time," but this is the closest he comes to acknowledging that the Soviet government had been given advance information by Churchill of the German intention to attack. Distortions deriving from political attitudes become more glaring as Platonov moves away from the strictly military aspects of the narrative.

The basic tendency of Stalinist historiography, as we have seen, was to deprecate the wartime roles of the professional military and the people, and to magnify the roles of Stalin and the party at their expense. After Stalin's death, the other elements of Soviet wartime society moved forward into the historical limelight, with the party taking the center of the stage. This arrangement of roles is basically retained in the present account, but Platonov's concentration on the specifically military aspects of the war has the effect of focussing attention on the role of the military in Soviet wartime achievements.

In this sphere he introduces details and refinements which constitute an innovation in the Soviet history of the war. The question of the basic command responsibility for the major military decisions of the war, for example, has always been a subject of imprecision in Soviet writing on the war. During Stalin's life, the "Supreme Commander" was identified as the author of all military decisions. After his death, the more impersonal "Supreme Command", or "General Headquarters" were often designated as the agencies of military initiative. With rare exceptions (including notably, General Eremenko's article in Military Thought, No. 3, 1949) military decisions were always presented as flowing from the top down, with front and army commanders playing no role in the formulation of these decisions. This obviously superficial picture of the complex processes of military decision-making began to be corrected in various accounts which came out from about 1955 on, and is completely discarded in Platonov's history. In place of it, he presents a fairly detailed discussion of how military plans were in fact formulated.

Regarding the plans for the Moscow counteroffensive, for example, he ascribes the initiative to Zhukov (without naming him), and the final product to the cooperative efforts of various top echelon commanders and staffs. "In accordance with the situation which had arisen," he writes, "the military Council of the Western Front presented a plan for a counteroffensive of the front to General Headquarters on November 30." Platonov then notes the additions to the plan introduced over the next few days, and concluded: "Thus, the plan for the counteroffensive under Moscow was the result of the great creative activity of the front commands, the General Staff, and the Headquarters of the Supreme Command." His account of the Stalingrad planning is approximately the same.

In a general appraisal of the lessons of the war at the end, Platonov discusses the wartime command processes in a more general way:

General Headquarters effected its leadership
through its representatives, staffs of directions,
the General Staff, the commanders and staffs of
specialized forces and troops, the central admin-
istrations of the Commissariat of Defense, the
commanders of fronts and fleets.... The strategic
leadership was not the same during the whole course
of the war. In the beginning of the war, the supreme commands of directions occupied a prominent
place in the leadership of the armed struggle.
From 1942, representatives of Headquarters of the
Supreme Command played an important role in the
leadership of the armed struggle in areas of military operations and strategic directions. In the
concluding campaigns of the Soviet troops in Europe
the Headquarters of the Supreme Command itself directed all the fronts, without sending its representatives to the place.

Platonov's history has its political padding which con-
tains, among other things, dutiful praise of the party's wartime leadership and of its mobilization of popular energies.
Like all post-Stalin accounts, too, it reflects the mozaic of
political forces in the current leadership. Khrushchev, for
example, is mentioned much more frequently than any other leader, and Zhukov is named only where historical decency requires.
But this padding is clearly distinguishable from the core of
the narrative, while depicts Soviet wartime society as a military machine in action, under the leadership appropriate to
such an organization.

The differentiation of approach to the military and political aspects of the war, which we have noted above, is demonstrated most clearly by Platonov's treatment of the role of
the Allies. In general the account is colored by deep hostility, but where military details are concerned, or, more particularly, where military lessons are to be drawn from the
history of Allied operations, Platonov does not hesitate to
face the facts.

The story of alleged Allied duplicity before and during
the war is recounted by Platonov much as it has always been told
in the Soviet Union. The Allies are depicted as having sought to
buy their own security before the war by encouraging Germany
to attack the Soviet Union. "The finale of this treachery,"

writes Platonov, "was the shameful Munich deal (sgovor) of the
English and French governments with Hitler, which gave Czecho-
slovakia to fascist Germany. It is completely obvious that
this was a recompense to Hitler for his undertaking to begin
war against the Soviet Union." In similar vein, Allied policy
during the war is interpreted as having been directed at the
exhaustion of the USSR and Germany and the extraction of max-
imum profits from the war.

The question of allied supplies to Russia during the war
is mentioned very sparingly by Platonov. The figures cited by
him are somewhat lower than those announced by the American
government, and Platonov does not explain the basis of his cal-
culations.

The expenditures of the USA on Lend-Lease supplies comprised 46.04 billion dollars, or 14% of the
total military expenditures of the USA. Of this sum,
the countries of the British Empire received goods
from the USA totaling 30.3 billion dollars (of which
England received 21.5 billion dollars), and the USSR
received the value of 10.8 billion dollars.

Thus, the Soviet Union which carried the major
burden of the war on its shoulders, and played the
decisive role in the victory of the anti-Hitlerite
coalition, received half as much under Lend-Lease as
England.

This unfairness affects also many aspects of Platonov's account of Allied military operations. He interprets Allied operations in Italy, for example, as aimed at the seizure of eastern
Europe, and he gives a very grudging appraisal of the Normandy
invasion. Where Allied and Soviet operations overlapped, as in
the protection of the Murmansk sea route, he grossly exaggerates
the Soviet role.

On the other hand, where he finds it useful to do so, Platonov presents data and observations which tend to contradict
these political interpretations. For example, in a section com-
paring the military potentials of the fascist and democratic
states before the war, Platonov cites many facts testifying to
the strenuous preparations of the democratic states for war in
the late 1930's, facts which tend to belie the Soviet claim that
these states were banking on a detente with Hitler and a Soviet-
German war. In another place, where he disparages the significance of Allied operations in Europe, he adds:

9 7 8 1 6 0 8 8 8 2 6 9 4